In *Can I Just Hide in* [...] [...]a Bolton and Christin [...] wisdom, hilarity, enc[...] practical advice, with a gentle reminder that everything's going to be all right. If you're tempted to hide under the covers because it's easier than facing life, consider reading this book. It'll infuse you with courage and confidence.

TWILA BELK
Speaker and author of *Raindrops from Heaven: Gentle Reminders of God's Power, Presence, and Purpose*

Don't miss this book! If you've ever struggled with life, faced fears, longed for better circumstances, dealt with discouragement, wondered how to find your joy, or needed to laugh out loud, read *Can I Just Hide in Bed 'til Jesus Comes Back?* Martha Bolton and Christin Ditchfield have combined their deep knowledge of biblical truth with their off-the-charts humor to write a book that will restore your hope, give you practical action steps, multiply your ability to see life as an adventure, and remind you not to take yourself too seriously. Buy one for yourself and ten more to give to your friends.

CAROL KENT
Speaker and author of *When I Lay My Isaac Down*

The title of this book asks the question that almost every woman has pondered at one time or another. Okay, I haven't actually thought about *hiding*; I've wanted to run away. But Martha Bolton and Christin Ditchfield are quick to point out that neither of those are good plans. Instead their delightful book encourages you to focus on what you *can* do—remember what is true: God loves you; He weeps with you; He equips you;

He defends you; He delivers you! So no hiding in bed! (And no running away.) Just curl up with this book and find the encouragement you need to move forward.

KENDRA SMILEY
Conference speaker and author of *Mother of the Year: 365 Days of Encouragement for Devoted Moms, Journey of a Strong-Willed Child*, and *Live Free: Eliminate the If Onlys and What Ifs of Life*

I'm a fan of anything Martha Bolton writes. Her words are always fresh, fun, engaging, and comforting—just like her. What she and Christin Ditchfield have created with *Can I Just Hide in Bed 'til Jesus Comes Back?* proves to be another winner. If you've struggled with fear, unworthiness, depression, or unfulfilled dreams, this is the book you need *now*. Martha and Christin show you how to crawl out of the hole and begin to live life in the fullness for which God created you. It came at the perfect time for me—my father's passing. This provided the comfort I needed and reminded me that God is still on the throne—even through the darkest of days.

SUSIE SHELLENBERGER
Creator of *Brio* magazine, author, and speaker

Can I Just Hide in Bed 'til Jesus Comes Back?

FACING LIFE WITH COURAGE, NOT COMFORTERS

Martha Bolton AND Christin Ditchfield

TYNDALE HOUSE PUBLISHERS, INC.
CAROL STREAM, ILLINOIS

FOCUS ON THE FAMILY®

Can I Just Hide in Bed 'til Jesus Comes Back? Facing Life with Courage, Not Comforters

© 2017 by Martha Bolton and Christin Ditchfield. All rights reserved.

A Focus on the Family book published by Tyndale House Publishers, Inc., Carol Stream, Illinois 60188

Focus on the Family and the accompanying logo and design are federally registered trademarks of Focus on the Family, 8605 Explorer Drive, Colorado Springs, CO 80920.

TYNDALE and Tyndale's quill logo are registered trademarks of Tyndale House Publishers, Inc.

Editor: Julie B. Holmquist
Cover design by Beth Sparkman
Cover illustration by Lindsey Bergsma. Copyright © Focus on the Family. All rights reserved.

For information about special discounts for bulk purchases, please contact Tyndale House Publishers at csresponse@tyndale.com, or call 1-800-323-9400.

Library of Congress Cataloging-in-Publication Data can be found at www.loc.gov.

ISBN 978-1-58997-924-6

Printed in the United States of America

23 22 21 20 19 18 17
7   6   5   4   3   2   1

Dedicated to
those who have lived in the shadow of fear,
weighed down by pain . . .
tangled up in discouragement, depression, or grief . . .
tempted to surrender in silence . . .
but bravely seeking the courage to face the world again.

Contents

Introduction

It's a dangerous business, Frodo, going out your door. You step into the Road, and if you don't keep your feet, there's no knowing where you might be swept off to.

BILBO BAGGINS in *The Fellowship of the Ring*

NEVER MIND STEPPING into the road. Sometimes stepping out of bed is dangerous enough—or daunting enough.

Yes, there are times when life can seem too hard to face.

There, we've said it. But you already know it's true. That's why you're holding this book. You already know that no matter how you try to motivate yourself, there are days when you wake up so overwhelmed or so discouraged, so hurt, angry, worried, or afraid, that it seems much safer and more comfortable to stay in bed. The world looks better from under the protective covering of a five-hundred-thread-count sheet or the comforting quilt hand stitched by your grandmother.

We've both been there.

We've found ourselves staying in bed and pulling the covers over our heads for all kinds of reasons. Sometimes it's just too scary out there. Too many things can go wrong. There's too much we can't control.

Sometimes it's too painful to throw back the covers. Look what happened last time! We were hurt, or someone we love was hurt. We were used or abused. Bullied. Battered. Betrayed. We tried and failed. We gave and they wanted more. We've been loved by some and kicked by others. Those wounds are still raw, the bruises still fresh. Isn't bed where you're supposed to be when you're healing? So what if it's been twelve years? Or twenty. Or forty. We shouldn't rush it, right?

Sometimes it's too embarrassing to face life. We'll only keep making mistakes. We'll trip over our feet, greet the boss with spinach in our teeth, and inadvertently wear our clothes with the tags still on them. We won't speak up when we need to, or we'll speak when we should be quiet. We'll only try and fail again.

Sometimes it's too overwhelming to climb out of bed. We just don't have the strength. The energy. The motivation.

If only we could get a good night's sleep!

Maybe you haven't been able to sleep either. You've been watching the hour hand on the clock ooze like slow lava from two to three to four o'clock in the morning. This is when you thank God for twenty-four-hour television and learn far more about the foreign markets and two-for-the-price-of-one kitchen gadgets than you ever wanted to know.

Once the sun rises, you might manage to gather up enough strength to face the day physically, only to discover that mentally, emotionally, and spiritually, you're still hiding under the covers. Your body may be at your job, or at your child's school or the grocery store, but your faith is back home enjoying its "sleep number."

Again, we know how you feel. We, too, have tried to survive days we'd rather not have on our calendars, convincing ourselves that "God will see us through," pretending we don't feel the crushing pain of whatever has disrupted our lives and destroyed our peace *this time*.

It's not easy. Some days it's practically impossible, isn't it? We may manage to get out of bed, putting one foot in front of the other, but we're still cowering under invisible blankets of fear, dread, and self-doubt. We're weighed down by feelings of worthlessness, a desperate need to please others, a protective distrust of unproven friendships, and more.

We try to play "nice," but instead of getting credit for it, we find our "niceness" is misinterpreted as weakness, or our timidity for aloofness. And weakness invites aggression. Timidity invites overlooking and discounting. We find ourselves being disregarded and taken advantage of more and more often. Endless people pleasing makes us feel invisible and disrespectful of our own needs and desires.

We figure we'll just stay out of everyone's way and not do anything significant with our lives, or not push back when we're walked on. After all, that would rock the boat and invite criticism, ridicule, and harassment. Just leave us alone to return to our bed caves and pick the down feathers out of our teeth.

Like you, we've each wrestled with the typical *who, what, when, where,* and *why* questions of life:

Who has so much free time that they feel the need to meddle in other people's pain?

What else can go wrong? Did the transmission have to go out the same day the stove stopped working and that check didn't come in the mail?

When is it going to stop? The problems keep piling on—one after another. And then that other one hops on just for the fun of it.

Where is a kind word, a helpful hand, a little appreciation, some encouragement? Helloooo? Where did everybody go?

Have you been there? We're sure you have.

And that brings us to *why*.

Why even bother getting out of bed? We have snacks. We

have Netflix. We'll just hide out in our beds until Jesus comes back. Why not? Hiding is the biblical thing to do.

Look at Adam and Eve: They hid from God after Eve disobeyed, and what price did they have to, um . . . scratch that. (It's a bad day when you lose the Garden of Eden.) What about Jonah? He ran away from what God had given him to do, and nothing happened to . . . wait, no. He did end up in the belly of a whale. What about David hiding from King Saul? David was on the run, hiding from his enemies, but also hiding from his own sin and failure; from grief and pain, loss and betrayal. And he was called a man after God's own heart. Why? Because David also did the *good* kind of hiding. He points us to the kind of hiding that actually *is* biblical:

> Show the wonder of your great love, you who save by your right hand those who take refuge in you. . . . Keep me as the apple of your eye; hide me in the shadow of your wings.
> PSALM 17:7-8

> You are my hiding place; you will protect me from trouble and surround me with songs of deliverance.
> PSALM 32:7

> In the day of trouble he will keep me safe in his dwelling; he will hide me in the shelter of his tabernacle and set me high upon a high rock.
> PSALM 27:5

> He who dwells in the shelter of the Most High will rest in the shadow of the Almighty. I will say of the LORD, "He is

my refuge and my fortress, my God, in whom I trust.". . .
He will cover you with his feathers, and under his wings
you will find refuge; his faithfulness will be your shield
and rampart.

PSALM 91:1-2, 4

There is a place to hide, but it's not under the covers. Or in the
broom closet. Or behind the hat of the lady sitting in front of
you in church. It's in the arms of our Father. His Spirit is the
Comforter we need to turn to in times of trouble. It's with Him
that we'll find peace and rest.

Of course, sometimes we may need a short respite to recover,
heal, and reenergize. After that, God's Word can get us back in
the action. We like this one:

Be on your guard; stand firm in the faith; . . . be strong.

1 CORINTHIANS 16:13

There are many Bible verses about standing firm. But it's hard to
stand firm on a mattress, isn't it? (We know. We've each tried in
our own homes. Your balance is off, and it's easy to trip and fall.
Plus, any injuries are a little embarrassing to explain in the ER.)
So clearly there must be a time for feet on the floor, a time to
put into practice those inspiring and empowering verses about
fighting the good fight, resisting the enemy, seizing the victory,
and advancing the Kingdom of God.

Again, all this is really hard to do with the covers stretched
over your head. We don't think any battlefield commander ever
traded in "Charge!" for "All right, troops, fluff your pillows,
hunker down for a nap, and then watch the enemy retreat!" You

might as well wave the white flag if that's as far as you'll go in thwarting the enemy.

We've learned that the hard way. Shivering on a pillow top mattress is no place for a soldier. There are better ways to deal with life's challenges than cowering in fear.

We can roll over and try to pretend the alarm clock isn't ringing and the hours of our lives aren't ticking away. But they are—and we need to pay attention. We need to get up and get going. Shake things up. Maybe even rock a few boats when necessary.

Jesus rocked a few boats in His day. He didn't hide under the covers when life got tough. He faced down the Pharisees and told parables challenging their "holier than thou" attitudes. He was no wimp or doormat. He faced the bullies, the self-righteous, and the "grizzly bears" of His day in His own humble yet firm way. He experienced pain and suffering, grief and loss. That didn't stop Him from getting about His Father's business. He knew His mission, and no one was able to deter Him from it. The same can be true for us.

We have walked up to doors, both physically and figuratively, and had them close in our face.

"Sorry."

"Wish I could help, but . . ."

"Maybe some other time."

"Our calendar is filled until December 2029."

We know that rejection is disappointing, frustrating, even heartbreaking. But the Bible tells us in Revelation 3:8, "See, I have placed before you an open door that no one can shut."

There are doors that God Himself has opened for us, and no one can close them. No one. Let the truth of that sink in. Naysayers can try to hinder us and convince us that the doors aren't open, that we're not worthy to walk through them, or that those doors were intended for someone else. They can try to fill us with fear and dread, try to put obstacles in our path, or try to convince others to help them block the doors. They might even try to push their way through the doors themselves. But they cannot shut them.

No one can stop a person from accomplishing what God has given him or her to accomplish.

Well, actually, there is *one* person.

The only one who can keep you trapped in doubt and inaction is yourself. The only one who can keep you from walking through the doors that God has opened for you is *you*.

Learning to face what we can't face in life is a hard choice. But while staying in bed—physically, emotionally, spiritually, metaphorically—might seem easy, safe, comfortable, or risk-free, it isn't. Most of the time, it only makes things worse. Who needs emotional bedsores?

While we're in bed, the problems just keep piling up along with the dishes and the laundry. Our strategy of self-protection backfires and somehow adds even more stress to our lives. The fear and dread . . . the guilt, embarrassment, and shame—even over things we never did . . . don't go away; they gang up on us.

We might feel safe in our bedrooms, but we're sentencing ourselves to a pretty miserable existence. Frankly, we've had enough of that kind of life. How about you?

It's your choice: You can give in to fear, discouragement, and defeat and stay in bed and pull the covers over your head until Jesus comes back.

Or you can learn to be bold, strong, and free.

Making that choice begins by taking that first step. Decide to get up, get dressed, and walk through that door. Get on with your life!

Whoa. Wait a minute. Easier said than done, right?

How do we get up, get dressed, and get going?

How do we get out of our emotional beds and leave our funk behind?

How do we face the realities we'd rather ignore, the disappointment of our unfulfilled longings, the pain of our abandoned hopes and dreams? How do we face our failures and mistakes, the people we've hurt and those who've hurt us? How do we accept that people we've been counting on aren't there for us? How do we deal with the loss and the grief?

Again, good news: Jesus Himself wants to pull back the covers of our threadbare protection, take us by the hand, and walk *with* us every step of the way.

We want to walk with you too!

Others do too.

You don't have to take a single step of this journey alone. None of us does.

PART ONE

Facing Your Feelings
When You'd Rather Hide

*If you can keep your head when all about you are losing theirs,
it's just possible you haven't grasped the situation.*

JEAN KERR

SOMETIMES WE FIND ourselves imprisoned by our fears. There are many to choose from: fear of risk; fear of change; fear of failure or rejection; fear of loss, death, or disaster. The list could go on and on.

We can find it hard to face our hurts, heartaches, and disappointments; the pain of regret, loss, missed opportunities, or poor choices. We'd rather not address our feelings of remorse, misplaced guilt, embarrassment, or blame. Sometimes we feel so frustrated, so angry, so powerless.

When we're feeling helpless and hopeless, bed may seem like a safer place to be. But like broken springs poking us in the middle of the night, pain will find us even there. There's a better choice!

In part one, we'll share what we've discovered about facing these powerful emotions. Learn with us about how to process your feelings, push through or past your fears, and press on!

CHAPTER I

SKIP THE SHEEP

Worry does not empty tomorrow of its sorrows; it empties today of its strength.

CORRIE TEN BOOM

My (Christin's) best friend teases me about being a princess—not the spunky, cute, Disney kind with an Academy Award–winning theme song, a cadre of charming forest friends, and a handsome prince—but the kind who lies on top of eighteen mattresses and loses sleep over a tiny green pea.

Sadly, it's true.

I've always envied people who can fall asleep at the drop of a hat. Midsentence even. People like my friend Cinderella (not her real name), who was so tired one day after work that she flopped on the bed for a minute at 5:30 p.m. and woke up at 7:30 the next morning!

Not me. I toss and turn, toss and turn, and turn and toss. I just can't seem to shut my mind off. I hear every tiny noise and notice changes in light, even with my eyes closed.

At the best of times, it's incredibly annoying to be generally happy with life and ready for rest and still have a hard time falling asleep.

At the worst of times, sleeplessness escalates to full-blown insomnia. My mind churns and churns and churns.

Since I can't fall asleep, and there's no one I want to chat with on Facebook, I do the next best thing: I worry.

I worry about how much sleep I'm losing and how tired I'm going to be in the morning. I check my cell phone (I used to check my alarm), telling myself, *If I fall asleep now, I could still get six hours . . . five hours . . . four hours . . . three full hours . . .*

I worry about the piles of laundry in the living room and dishes in the sink. The food going bad in the fridge. The leaky roof. The funny sound the car's been making. The funny sound my bones have been making.

I worry about the piles of bills on my desk and the empty account at my bank.

I think of family members and friends who are in various crises and feel helpless that there doesn't seem to be anything I can do to solve their problems. If only I had money to give them, or a car, or a house, or energy. If only I could give their "ex" or their boss or their ungrateful teen a piece of my mind on their behalf. If only I could give their doctors wisdom, or better yet, heal them myself!

But I can't even fix myself!

That realization leads me to thoughts of what's wrong in my life.

I relive humiliating moments, mistakes I've made, and wounds I've suffered. You know—the "shoulda, coulda, woulda" stuff coupled with those "didn't want it, didn't deserve it, and didn't see it coming" moments.

I practice the clever and witty points I wish I could have made, the comments I tell myself I'll express next time. (Even though I won't. Not really. Oh, but I do sound articulate and convincing in my mind.)

I ruminate on my to-do list, trying to figure out how I can possibly do it all. I feel guilty about what I didn't do the day before and promise myself I'll catch up tomorrow. (Then I feel guilty for lying to myself, because I know myself too well.)

The to-do list is filled with unpleasant stuff: sorting out that insurance mess, answering one hundred e-mails, making decisions about this, finding a solution for that. It's overwhelming.

Even when I do finally fall asleep, it's a restless sleep. All it takes is a cricket sneezing half a mile away, and I'm back to tossing and turning again (and fantasizing about hunting down the poor critter to gag him!).

All too soon morning comes, and I can't face it. I just want to stay in bed and pull the covers over my head.

Count on the Shepherd

That's the scenario, unless I make a conscious decision to turn off the noise in my head and turn on the blinding light instead.

Literally. (Ow!)

I turn on my bedside table lamp and reach for my Bible and my prayer journal. Sometimes I play praise and worship music or an audio recording of Scripture or Scripture-based prayers.

On my bed I remember you; I think of you through the watches of the night. Because you are my help, I sing in the shadow of your wings.

PSALM 63:6-7

> Do not worry about tomorrow, for tomorrow will worry about itself. Each day has enough trouble of its own.
>
> MATTHEW 6:34

I've never fallen asleep counting sheep, but I've often found great comfort and peace talking to the Shepherd.

And it's amazing how quickly sleep comes when you try to spend an hour in prayer!

> I will lie down and sleep in peace, for you alone, O LORD, make me dwell in safety.
>
> PSALM 4:8

Now I lay me down to fret,
to toss and turn—did I forget
that God is here right by my side?
No need to worry. No need to hide.

CHAPTER 2

BREAKING MURPHY'S LAW

Everything you want is on the other side of fear.
GEORGE ADDAIR

WHEN I (CHRISTIN) WAS A CHILD, I was a voracious reader. A trip
to the library took at least three hours: two to make my initial
selections, and then another hour to painstakingly trim the pile
to the thirty-book checkout limit.

At home, I read and reread my favorites until they fell apart,
and then, often out of sheer boredom, I read anything and everything else I could get my hands on—cereal boxes, dictionaries,
encyclopedias, women's magazines full of advice to harried
housewives, even self-help and motivational books intended for
salesmen. You name it, I read it. (Video games had been invented
back then, but they were housed in arcades, cost a quarter a turn,
and were mostly played by pesky, little-brother types.)

I remember one day rifling through a parent or grandparent's
desk drawer, desperate for new material, and stumbling across

a flip calendar that featured a cartoon raccoon. It looked kid-friendly, but the snarky sayings for each month caught me off guard and cracked me up:

If anything can go wrong, it will.

The bread always falls jam-side down.

You never find whatever you lost until you replace it.

And this classic:

The light at the end of the tunnel may be the headlight of an oncoming train.

I had a bit of a sarcastic streak, and I thought these "laws" were hilarious. And somehow, they resonated with me. So I read the calendar over and over until I had memorized them.

In hindsight, that may have been a mistake.

I look back now and realize that I've spent much of my life waiting for things to go wrong, expecting the bread to fall jam-side down.

On some level I think this attitude is part of my God-given personality, the way He's wired me to see patterns, to consider the future, to anticipate, predict, and problem-solve. I always ask, "What could possibly go wrong?" And then I do what I can to prevent it, to protect myself and the people I love from that outcome. It can be a strength, a gift.

But it's not such a good thing when I focus exclusively on what *could* go wrong, or when I allow myself to be convinced that it *will* go wrong instead of focusing on what's already good and right, and what can be strengthened, improved, or accomplished.

It's not a good thing when it takes my eyes off the God who loves me and gave Himself for me, the One who promised He would never leave me nor forsake me. It's not good when I forget to focus only on what He's asked of me.

And as for convincing yourself that the light at the end of the tunnel is almost always attached to an oncoming train? That kind of mentality will quickly rob you of peace and ruin your health and happiness.

It will sabotage your success. That's important to remember.

Anticipating a train wreck can land us in bed. Fear can freeze us into believing that our dream, what God has called us to achieve, is out of our reach. And fear of success can also make us burrow deeper under the covers. We're afraid to achieve a dream because if we do, our new status will be way too hard to handle. Or we don't deserve it in the first place, so why even bother?

We tell ourselves that success means . . .

More work.
More problems.
More responsibilities.
Greater stakes.
Greater opportunities to fail more spectacularly, and in front of a larger audience.

And some of that is unfortunately true. It goes with the territory. But those factors alone shouldn't stand in the way of our striving to be faithful to God's calling and be the best we can be. Yes, there is a price for success. But complacency and apathy come with a hefty price tag too—a life filled with disappointment, frustration, and regret.

We say if you're going to pay a price for inaction as well as action, why not choose action?

Don't anticipate or assume the worst. Don't allow yourself to believe that failure is your lot in life. And don't fear success when you see it barreling toward you. Don't get out of its way or hide in the shadows until it passes by. Jump on board and embrace the adventure. And remember what God says in Jeremiah 29:11: "'I know the plans I have for you,' declares the LORD, 'plans to prosper you and not to harm you, plans to give you hope and a future.'"

Top Ten Excuses, Er, Reasons, for Staying in Bed

10. I'm seeking the Lord in a dream.
9. I'm lying prostrate in total surrender.
8. I'm using the ceiling tiles to count off each of my blessings.
7. The pillows over my face help me concentrate on biblical matters.
6. I'm testing out the quilts before mailing them off to the missionaries.
5. I'm being a good steward and not wearing out the feet in my pajamas.
4. The Bible says "be still," and I just want to be a "doer of the Word."
3. I'm resting in the Lord. And resting. And resting.
2. The less contact I have with the outside world, the more spiritual I am. It's easier to love people if you don't have to deal with them.
1. When Jesus comes back, He'll know right where to find me—and I'll already be wearing my robe!

CHAPTER 3

STARING DOWN THE MONSTER IN THE CLOSET

Fear makes the wolf bigger than he is.
GERMAN PROVERB

THERE ARE MANY REASONS to stay in bed. But we think one of the best ones is remaining within reach of the chocolate chip cookies hidden behind the headboard.

Now, we don't have a scientific chart that tells you exactly how many chocolate chip cookies it takes to face your fear, but if we were to venture a guess, we would say most ordinary fears need about two or three. Medium fears might require three or more, along with a glass of milk. Major fears could call for an entire bag, chunky chocolate style with marshmallows.

They tell us we're supposed to face our fears, right? Look whatever we're afraid of straight in the eye and not back down. But who in their right mind would ever stare down that "monster in the closet"?

Surely, it's only your winter jacket hanging precariously on the door hanger, next to the birthday balloon with just a bit of helium left inside. But it appears a far more threatening creature as you're peeking out from under the covers (the shivering doesn't help your focus either).

Stare him down? No way!

Yet that *is* what we need to do. Why? So we can see the size of the monster, for one thing. (If he's only three feet tall, I can take him.) And so we can see if the thing we're fearing is actually what we think it is.

One time, I (Martha) got up in the middle of the night to get a drink of water. I didn't bother turning on the kitchen light because the moonlight bouncing off the Ding Dongs wrappers above the refrigerator illuminated the room quite nicely.

I walked over to the sink, grabbed a glass, and started filling it with water. Suddenly, in the darkness, a voice boomed out in the still of the night.

"What are you looking at?"

I nearly dropped my glass in panic. It was definitely a man's voice, and he was not a member of my family. Or anyone else I knew for that matter. I froze.

Once again, he called out, "What are you looking at?" The tone and inflection were exactly the same. Just as forceful and just as creepy. I tried to scream, but no sound came out.

Then the intruder continued, "Haven't you ever seen a talking fish before?"

I started to tell him no, but my better sense told me not to converse with the man who was . . . wait a minute! I turned on the lights and caught him red-handed.

My intruder was a talking fish plaque that one of our sons had given to his dad several years prior. Its batteries had long since died, and we had forgotten all about it. That is, until it suddenly decided to scare me half to death in the middle of the night in that dark kitchen!

That fish taught me something. I've learned it helps to shine a light on your fear—or *the* Light, for that matter. Make sure your fear isn't just a talking fish in the dark.

That memory reminds me of another sleepless night I once spent shaking because I was scheduled to speak about comedy writing the following morning at a conference with fellow Bob Hope writer Gene Perret.

Being naturally shy, standing on stage and speaking to an audience was not an experience I sought. But I said I'd do it, so I was determined to keep my promise.

Hundreds of people were attending the event, and of course, they were all professional speakers. Not only was I going to bomb, I was going to do it grandly!

I tried to sleep in my hotel room, but my nervous shaking kept me (and my husband) awake. Finally, I climbed out of bed and paced the floor. And paced. And paced. Hour after hour passed. I asked myself, *What's the worst that could happen?*

I could pass out. The audience could throw things at me. I could break down and cry for my mommy. I could never be invited to speak again. Anywhere. Ever. On the other hand, I could do fine, or be simply adequate, or at least not horrible. But that wasn't likely. And so I paced.

I honestly saw no way out of this sure failure. My husband and I had traveled there, I was announced on their printed program as a speaker, and my cowriter was counting on me to share the stage with him. What else could I do?

That's it! I thought.

I could tell him I was sick, which I was, and I was feeling more ill with each passing minute. I could say I had to rush home for a family emergency. And actually, there was someone in the family who needed urgent help—*me!*

Unfortunately neither of those plans would work, because I would still be letting down my friend. So I paced. And I shook. And I stressed. And I worried.

Finally, at the crack of dawn, I made a decision. I would simply tell Gene my fears, how I'd stayed up all night worrying, and beg for his mercy and understanding.

To my surprise when I called him, he couldn't have been more gracious. He felt terrible that I had stayed up all night feeling stressed over the matter. He happily agreed to do the talk on his own, and we've since shared plenty of laughs about the incident.

My fear, as real as it was that night, was something that I would eventually conquer. And when I did give public speaking another try, you know what? Not one of the things I feared happened. I didn't pass out, no one threw anything at me, and I didn't once cry for my mother. (Not out loud, anyway.)

If the Timid Made Road Signs

Road signs have to be definitive. They can't beat around the bush. People's lives are at stake. So it might not be a good idea for the timid to make road signs. They could end up sounding like this:

Do Not Enter
We really sort of almost mean this.

One Way
You pick which one.

Stop
If it works into your plans.

Speed Limit 45
Not enough? We can negotiate.

Exit Now
Or whenever you're "feeling" it.

Yield
(Of course. What else would the timid do?)

Dead End
Or wait. Maybe it's just sick.

Merge with Traffic
Can't we all just get along?

No Passing
How will the other cars feel?

Bridge Out
We would have told you sooner, but we didn't want to bother you.
Hope you can swim.

CHAPTER 4

MAYBE THE SKY *ISN'T* FALLING

I am an old man and have known a great many troubles, but most of them have never happened.

ATTRIBUTED TO MARK TWAIN

THE WILD-EYED WOMAN gestured vigorously at the sky as she described to the news reporter how, earlier in the day, she'd been standing in her yard, minding her own business, when the airplane part had plummeted from the sky and barely missed her.

Can you imagine her shock when she looked up and saw that chunk of metal descending toward her?

How do you prepare for something like that?

(If you know, please e-mail us. We like to be ready for anything and everything.)

We looked, and there isn't an app for that.

Seriously, nothing can prepare you for that kind of freakish disaster or the possibility of the dozens (if not hundreds) of others that occur around the world every day. You can't walk around wearing a football helmet or construction hard hat 24-7. (Think how your hair would look in all those selfies your BFF insists on taking, then tagging and memorializing you on Facebook forever.)

Who wants that kind of an existence?

You just can't live in fear. Consider the odds of something like that ever happening to you (we mean the "airplane part falling from the sky" scenario, not the "bad hair day memorialized on social media by overenthusiastic friends" thing, which is an all-too-common phenomenon, unfortunately).

Until we see falling-debris-repellant jackets, hats, and hoodies being marketed on QVC, we've concluded we shouldn't lose much sleep over that possibility. It's probably safe to step outside and go on with our lives.

If you don't believe us, believe the people who conducted research and surveys and then performed complicated, in-depth analyses, determining that of all the things we fear, approximately

- forty percent will never happen;
- thirty percent have already happened (things in the past you can't change or undo);
- twelve percent are health-related (ironic, since worry aggravates most health issues); and
- ten percent are petty, random, miscellaneous.[1]

That leaves only 8 percent of fears based on legitimate issues, which we'd have more focus and energy to address if we weren't wasting time on the 70 percent that have already happened or never will occur!

No wonder Will Rogers once said, "Worrying is like paying on a debt that may never come due."

But it's not easy to resist the temptation. We think a steady diet of constantly "breaking stories" on the twenty-four-hour TV news channels and the distressing reports that show up in our social media feeds would make even the most optimistic soul feel anxious and send her climbing back into bed:

"Stock Market Tanks!"

"Mystery Illness Sweeps the Nation!"

"Justin Bieber Elected President."

"Violin Spider in Teapot Kills Six!"

And then there are those Internet "warnings" that appear without, well, warning, and disturb what might have been an otherwise peaceful day:

"Three Signs Your Elbows Are Prematurely Aging You."

"Hidden Dangers Lurking in Your Sofa Cushions."

"Surprising Places Spiders Hide on Airplanes!"

If you've ever fallen for a hoax or urban legend, you know the fear it can cause until you realize it's false, or at the very least, completely overblown.

The only things we *have* found in our seat cushions are old candy and loose change (both of which we're quite happy about). Our elbows aren't aging us; it's our birthdays (though when we consider the alternative, we're not complaining). And we've flown plenty of miles over the years without seeing a single spider onboard (even now, with in-flight access to the World Wide *Web*).

Sometimes even the real news stories turn out to be far less scary or threatening than the headlines would lead us to believe. The stock market didn't tank; it just dipped. The mystery illness doesn't sweep the nation; it strikes only a handful of people, and they recover quickly. Justin Bieber is Canadian—he can't be elected president of this country. He's probably not interested in the job anyway. And everyone knows violin spiders prefer coffee to tea.

Worry too much about this stuff and you could make yourself

sick. Wait! Forget we said that. We don't want you worrying about your health too.

Have you ever had the occasion to spend much time around a hypochondriac? Granted, people with this disorder can't help it, but spending time around them is draining. Whatever the "disease du jour" is, they are sure they have it. Bless their hearts; they spend so much time in the ER they could have their mail delivered there.

We're talking about the ones who check every box on their medical history form as if it were a sushi menu and they were placing an order.

Impacted wisdom tooth? Hmmm . . . I'll take two.

Hemorrhoids? I think I'll sit that one out.

Eczema? Maybe as a starter.

High blood pressure? I'm still deciding. I'll probably go with that or the uncontrollable eye twitch. Can I let you know by Friday?

The sad thing is that people with this anxiety disorder, or those who simply crave the attention, worry about diseases they *don't* have instead of being able to enjoy the good health they *do* have.

Our health is going to fail someday. Unless we die in an accident, we can be sure of that. My (Martha's) father always used to say, "None of us are getting out of this world alive." It's true.

But as Mark Twain said, most of the troubles we feared would come upon us never did. Not the big ones anyway. Here are just a few of my "Didn't Happens":

- I didn't fall into the Grand Canyon.
- I didn't miss the last flight out of New York just before a historic blizzard was due to hit.
- I didn't watch a loved one struggle through a crisis without encouragement. Someone *did* come along and offer

encouragement. Not the people I would have expected to do it, but God made sure the encouragement came through someone.

- Our car didn't need a new transmission.
- The check didn't come late.
- I didn't feel alone, because a faithful friend had my back.

Bottom line: There's no reason to panic. Maybe the sky really isn't falling. Most likely, your situation isn't the end of the world. It just feels like it.

When you recognize that churning-in-the-gut feeling, stop and reassess the problem. Gather the facts. Talk to a trusted friend or counselor who can help you process the situation clearly. Consider the wise words of Mr. Rogers (Fred):

> Anything that's human is mentionable, and anything that is mentionable can be more manageable. When we can talk about our feelings, they become less overwhelming, less upsetting, and less scary. The people we trust with that important talk can help us know that we are not alone.[2]

After talking with someone about the situation, decide if you can feasibly do something about it, and if so, act.

If the sky really *is* falling, you can't do much more than try to stay out of harm's way until everything settles and someone puts the sky back where it belongs.

But for the record:

God is still on His throne. And the sky hasn't fallen to date.

> For by him all things were created: things in heaven and on earth, visible and invisible. . . . All things were created

by him and for him. He is before all things, and in him all things hold together.

COLOSSIANS 1:16-17

The Media-Lite Diet for Inner Peace

- Only one serving of politics per day. Partial fasting may be necessary during an election year due to the high risk of stress eating and stomach ulcers. (But informed voting is allowed and encouraged.)
- Do not exceed more than three servings of infomercials in a twenty-four-hour period.
- Radio talk shows should only be "enjoyed" by persons whose blood pressure needs elevating.
- Watch all competitive sports in moderation, except for golf and chess, which count as rest because of the prime nap time between actual play.
- Shopping networks make for good side dishes, but be careful. They can give your budget that bloated feeling.
- Animal shows are fine, unless they feature spiders.
- Do-it-yourself shows are not allowed for people with more than fifty DIY projects still in progress.
- Inspirational shows and movies are free calories! Enjoy and be inspired.

CHAPTER 5

DON'T MISS THE ADVENTURE

One way to get the most out of life is to look upon it as an adventure.
WILLIAM FEATHER

HAVE YOU EVER LET your fear stop you from having an adventure?

Once when I was appearing on a television show being taped in Canada, I (Martha) had some free time before my return flight home. Since Niagara Falls was close by, I wanted to see it. The weather was frigid—below zero with the windchill factor— and I was traveling alone. These were perfectly good reasons for me to stay cozied up in my warm hotel room. But I *really* wanted to see the Falls.

I vacillated between feeling courageous and thinking, *Are you nuts? It's cold out there.* Then came all the what-ifs. What if I get lost? What if I get sick? What if I freeze into an ice sculpture? What if I drop my purse over the Falls, or my camera? What if *I* slip and fall over? What if the gift shop is closed?

I think I had processed my way through every possible scenario

CAN I JUST HIDE IN BED 'TIL JESUS COMES BACK?

by the time I finally made my decision to throw caution to the wind. I boarded the bus that took me partway and caught a taxi to the Falls.

I did have to stand outside in the cold for a short time while waiting for the taxi, but then I reached my destination and walked around the Falls in the falling snow. Yes, I was freezing, I was alone, and I was fearful of slipping on the ice.

But what awaited me was one of the most spectacular sights I've ever seen. Niagara Falls in the winter is breathtaking!

When I finally made it back to my hotel, I took a nice hot bath and warmed up. I drank hot tea and warmed up. And I added some extra blankets to my bed and warmed up. I had been cold and scared, but I had seen the Falls! I had even mustered the courage to ask some strangers to take my photo there.

I was proud of myself. I had looked fear in the face and didn't allow it to stop me from making a memory I will never forget. There's nothing like a moment when you know you've charged at fear head-on and knocked it out!

As one of the timid, I realize that our bodies experience a physical reaction to fear, not just an emotional one. Even when we try our best to veil it, it can be quite obvious. We may physically shake; our stomachs churn, our voices tremble or rise an octave, and we turn pale. We have to talk ourselves out of running back to our safe and happy place. Even if that happy place is just in our minds.

Helen Keller once said, "Security is mostly a superstition. It does not exist in nature, nor do the children of men as a whole experience it. Avoiding danger is no safer in the long run than outright exposure. Life is either a daring adventure or nothing."[3]

These words of wisdom come not from a dismissed CEO who is now investing his $1.2 million golden parachute. No, these words come from a woman who faced many personal fears, challenges, and obstacles—and conquered them!

If anyone had an excuse to stay in bed, it was Helen. After all, she was born blind and deaf. Many of us know about her early life, and we realize that learning to speak sign language was a monumental accomplishment.

But most of us don't know of Helen's incredible feats following that communication breakthrough. She went on to become the first blind and deaf woman to attend college and earn a bachelor's degree. In her own lifetime, Helen was a famous author, an activist, and a lecturer who traveled to countries all over the world having daring adventures.

Don't let fear keep you from your adventure. Exciting experiences await you!

Life Lessons Learned from Ice Cream

1. Sometimes licking a "Rocky Road" can lead to "Cherries Jubilee"!
2. Even brain freeze passes eventually.
3. Life, like ice cream, can occasionally get messy.
4. Sorry, but you may have to maneuver your way around some nuts.
5. If you only pay attention to the top, you might miss what's dripping in other areas.
6. When your triple tower of delight tumbles to the ground, don't give up. You've still got the cone. Build on it again!
7. Sometimes the hardest decision is among thirty-one good things. When there's no bad choice, it's simply up to you.
8. Chocolate really does make things better.

9. You may be anxious to slurp up every scoop of life, but too much (even of a good thing) all at once can make you nauseous.

10. And finally, when you start to feel overwhelmed, remember the greatest lesson learned from ice cream: *Just chill.*

CHAPTER 6

SHELTER IN PLACE

Never be afraid to trust an unknown future to a known God.
CORRIE TEN BOOM

SOME OF US ARE OLD ENOUGH to remember a time during the Cold War era when our schoolteachers conducted surprise safety drills during class. We were told to crouch under our desks, curl up with our hands clasped over our heads, and wait for the signal that it was okay to come out, get back in our seats, and continue with our classwork.

How did we ever learn division or memorize spelling lists after the sudden, terrifying reminder that bombs could be dropped on us at any time, in the now-dubious safety of our schools?

Today, breaking news announcements of the latest school shootings penetrate our peace and have our minds racing to prayer for our own children or grandchildren, as well as for those experiencing the events.

Perhaps you've had to take cover as you've been deeply affected—even traumatized—by the recent events unfolding across our country and around the world.

Or maybe you've faced a time in your life when you felt you needed to take *emotional* cover. You ran to hide under your desk mentally or spiritually, if not physically.

You may not have known when the bombs would drop; no one was yelling, "Incoming . . . two o'clock!" You may not have known the identity or the exact location of the enemy, but you knew you were under attack. And when it was over, the destruction was everywhere around you.

At that point, you may have assessed the damage, become overwhelmed, and done the only thing you knew how to do—close the blinds and climb back into bed where life used to be so much more comfortable and safe.

Problem is, though, you're still there.

Long after the all-clear signal has been issued, you're still hunkered down, curled up in the fetal position and waiting for more assurances that something terrible isn't about to happen again.

Getting back on your feet isn't a guarantee that something else won't happen, but staying down isn't either.

Think about it: If there ever is a nuclear disaster, is hiding under the covers going to help all that much? We don't know of any blanket that thick.

So what can we do?

So many circumstances are beyond our control. Take nuclear war, for example. None of us has a missile defense system in our backyard ready to knock down a nuclear warhead. We have garden hoses, but the water doesn't shoot that high. And throwing pink flamingo lawn ornaments at an incoming missile is hardly going to make a dent in it. In either the missile or the flamingo. We'd probably just miss anyway.

Nor do we control the economy. Sure, we can help keep it healthy by being good American consumers during our back-to-school or Christmas shopping sprees. But ultimately we must admit that our influence on the world's financial situation is limited.

In all seriousness, we can do our best to live as wisely as possible and make the best decisions we can under whatever circumstances we're facing, but we can't prepare for things beyond our control.

Worrying about such out-of-our-control things is a waste of time and energy. We don't have control of the uncertainties in our lives—or our loved ones' lives, either. Things happen—difficult things, hard-to-understand things, things we didn't want and didn't need, the thing we feared, or the thing we never imagined.

How do we keep from staying curled up and under the covers?

First, we deliberately remember times when God delivered us from danger and walked us through fearful places, never once letting go of our hands.

Second, we remind ourselves that our hope is in the Lord, not in our ability to predict, prevent, or problem-solve every possible outcome.

And third, we ask God to fill our hearts with His perfect peace. We intentionally, purposefully place our trust in the One who holds our future in His hands.

He who dwells in the shelter of the Most High will rest in the shadow of the Almighty. I will say of the LORD, "He is my refuge and my fortress, my God, in whom I trust.

PSALM 91:1-2

CHAPTER 7

SHORT-SHEETED

All men make mistakes, but only wise men learn from their mistakes.
WINSTON CHURCHILL

HAVE YOU EVER COUNTED the threads in your sheets? The package lists a thread count of five hundred, but is that count truly accurate? Maybe you have those softer ones, say one thousand thread count or more. You wouldn't lie in bed counting each thread just to make sure the manufacturer got it right, would you? That would be like counting staples. Do you really have that much free time on your hands?

Of course not. You've got better things to do. You simply trust the manufacturer.

Why is it, then, that we have to know every "thread" of what happens in our lives?

Why did this or that go wrong? Where did I, he, she, they get off track? Why can't I catch a break? How did we end up here, stuck in this miserable situation? Who is to blame?

Thread after thread after thread, we go through our lives counting and re-counting and re-counting some more.

What does it get us? It doesn't change anything. If we purchased the sheets, then we knew what was in the package. We had the thread-count information and used it to make what we thought was the best decision at the time.

But what if we didn't choose the sheets? What if they were chosen for us?

Or worse yet, what if the package advertised a high thread count, but the sheets turned out to be only two hundred? We were blindsided, duped, misled, swindled, and now we're lying on this scratchy, hard "sheet" of life through no fault of our own, doomed to an endless string of sleepless nights, right?

Wrong! Absolutely wrong! We have a choice to surrender or stand.

In John 5:6, Jesus asks a paralyzed man lying by the pool, "Do you want to get well?" The man replies by complaining about his unfair circumstances and all the obstacles he is facing.

But Jesus doesn't enter into the blame game or debate the man's difficulties or disadvantages. He offers healing with these simple words: "Take up your mat and walk!"

To those of us not just wounded but also wallowing in our misery, this same Jesus offers healing along with a little tough love: "Get up!"

Stop counting those scratchy threads—replaying the negative messages, reliving the worst experiences, rehearsing your grievances.

Stop playing the blame game—listing all the reasons and excuses, no matter how legitimate.

Change the sheets of exhaustion, discouragement and despair, self-pity, fear, remorse, and regret. Get down to Bed, Bath &

Beyond Yourself and pick out a new package of bed sheets, woven with thousands of threads of gratitude, amazing grace, new mercies every morning, fresh confidence, faith, and trust. Not to mention priceless wisdom from all the lessons learned.

You'll soon find the energy and strength to walk into your future with your well-rested head held high.

Top Ten Least Helpful Things Ever Said to the Bedridden

(We can't say for certain, but we think these immortal words were first uttered by Job's friends.)

10. Move that IV so I can sit down and tell you about *my* problems.
9. This, too, shall pass. But until then, lighten up, would you? You're bringing us all down.
8. I know you're in pain, but keep the moaning down, would you please? My shows are on.
7. Shouldn't you be over this by now? It's been like an hour already.
6. If you'd listened to me in the first place, none of this would have happened.
5. I wish *I* could just stay in bed all day!
4. All my problems were solved when I started taking these nutritious, holistic, all-natural, multilevel-marketing-company supplements. I'll sign you up today.
3. Wow! Have you looked in a mirror lately?
2. You know, there are better ways to get attention.
1. Seriously, what's *wrong* with you?

CHAPTER 8

IT'S GOING TO BE ALL RIGHT

I believe in the sun even when it isn't shining. I believe in love even when I don't feel it. I believe in God even when He is silent.

CARVED INTO A CELLAR WALL WHERE JEWS HID DURING THE HOLOCAUST

WHEN MY (MARTHA'S) SISTER MELVA had been diagnosed with uterine cancer and was going through chemotherapy, she didn't know what her future held. She prayed for God to heal her, but she also knew the road ahead would be challenging.

Instead of reaching for typical books of encouragement, she found comfort in reading books about others who had faced horrific challenges and somehow managed to keep their fears in check, drawing from the peace and power only God could have given. She read about the Holocaust survivors, as well as survivors of the Rwandan genocide, and drew strength from the courage of these unbelievably brave souls. She told herself if they could face what they had to face and not lose hope, then she could face cancer. Their stories, as heart-wrenching as they were, gave her courage, renewed her hope, and increased her faith.

Whose story inspires you and helps get you through your day? Think of someone whose perseverance and faith reminds you that . . .

It's going to be all right.

These six simple words are easy to say; there's not a single tongue-twisting syllable among them. Yet they seem too simplistic to actually do any good, don't they? They could come across as trite, so we sometimes talk ourselves out of saying them to someone else.

It's too bad, because that phrase may be exactly what someone needs to hear.

"It's going to be all right."

This statement isn't an assurance of no more pain, medical procedures, bills, sleepless nights, bad news, or disappointments. It doesn't promise a future without a new normal. It means this: If we know Jesus, we can trust that He'll use our circumstances for good. Someday, somehow, some way. That's the *all right* that we're talking about.

Scripture tells us that "in all things God works for the good of those who love him" (Romans 8:28). Not that all things *are* good, but that *in* all things God works for our good. In other words . . .

It's going to be all right.

I can recall many times in my life when those words kept me hanging on, allowing me to push through my doubts and fears.

I remember that when I was first diagnosed with diabetes, I asked for prayer. I didn't know what my future held. I had grown up watching my older sister, who was diagnosed with diabetes at age four, cope with the disease. I witnessed a series of frightening episodes of hypoglycemia and hyperglycemia. She was in and out of hospitals regularly, and too often as I was walking home from school, I would turn the corner and see an ambulance in front of my house.

The news of my own diabetes was not welcome. As it turned out, our church had a special guest speaker who happened to be a medical doctor. So I asked that man to pray for me. He did, and then he looked at me, saying, "It's going to be all right."

I cannot tell you how comforting those words were to hear, and how many times throughout my life I have replayed them in my head. When my sister's diabetes caused complications leading to her premature death at forty-four, I repeated those words to myself:

It's going to be all right.

As a family we grieved deeply the tragic loss of her young life. But she had always faced her disease with courage, and to her, heaven was the ultimate "all right." But her death also didn't mean that I was inescapably fated to die young too.

I have now lived more than forty years with diabetes and continue to keep a full work schedule. It hasn't slowed me down. I've been unconscious only once, and that was because it had been a stressful day and I had gone to bed early without eating enough. The next time I opened my eyes, I was surrounded by my family and paramedics.

It's going to be all right, I told myself, remembering that speaker's words.

Other times when those words were either spoken to me or I said them to myself, they gave me the strength and encouragement to keep going.

How about you? Has someone spoken those words into your life? Or are there people around you who need to hear that good news?

You may have to face your greatest fears. You may have to

endure loss, grief, or pain. Things may change; you may have to learn to live in a new way.

But it's going to be all right. God's in control, and nothing is going to happen that He won't see you through. He's promised you that.

> Who shall separate us from the love of Christ? Shall
> trouble or hardship or persecution or famine or nakedness
> or danger or sword? . . . No, in all things we are more
> than conquerors through him who loved us. For I am
> convinced that neither death nor life, neither angels
> nor demons, neither the present nor the future, nor any
> powers, neither height nor depth, nor anything else in
> all creation, will be able to separate us from the love of
> God that is in Christ Jesus our Lord.
>
> ROMANS 8:35, 37-39

CHAPTER 9

IT ONLY HURTS
WHEN I BREATHE

Life is pain. . . . Anyone who says differently is selling something.
MAN IN BLACK, IN *The Princess Bride*

"YOU'RE THE ONLY PATIENT I've ever seen who's had this reaction."

"I've never operated on anyone before who's had these kinds of complications."

"You're my one failure!"

If I (Christin) had a dollar for every time a doctor has said something like this to me, I'd be able to pay my medical bills.

I've learned the hard way that staying in bed for real is not nearly as fun or as restful as it sounds.

It's a long story that I don't plan to start telling in detail until I'm in a nursing home or without cable TV. But it involves (among other things) chronic pain, eight or nine major surgeries, bone grafts and horrifically long metal screws, an artificial joint, and three full years (spread out across five) on crutches, including eight months in one calendar year when I fancy-fractured my leg not once, but twice.

"Fancy" meaning I didn't do anything: It just broke. Fancy that. And then it broke again. My doctor was trying to be reassuring (I think) when he told me I'm lucky to be living in the age of MRIs because some fractures are so fancy, they don't show up on X-rays. He says they used to think people like me were imagining things and would pass us off to psychiatrists!

Lovely.

Through the years, sweet people who mean well have suggested to me that God must want me to rest and relax and enjoy some time away from my busy schedule.

But I've found that staying in bed when you are in pain is not particularly restful or relaxing.

Your busy schedule, bills, responsibilities, and obligations don't disappear. You don't magically inherit a fortune, a personal assistant, and household staff.

Your bed can quickly feel like a prison, even *with* a stack of takeout menus, a subscription to Netflix, a bucket of pain pills, and a handy grabber for the stuff you drop on the floor.

I've also learned that pain and suffering don't automatically cause a person to exhibit great strength of character, spiritual growth, or intimacy with God. When I was a child, I thought they did, and—wait for it—I wished something bad would happen to me!

Back then, I was moved by all the stories I read of great men and women of faith who overcame seemingly insurmountable obstacles to do great things for God. I wanted to have that kind of depth, that kind of richness in my relationship with Him.

Imagine my disappointment when I discovered that pain doesn't make me spiritual—it makes me cranky. Crabby.

Irritable. It shows me just how selfish and whiny and self-pitying I can be. Ugh.

I've learned that while staying in bed can allow some things to heal, it can damage others. The bone in my leg might be healing, but the unused muscle is now hanging there, a shriveled, miserable-looking thing. It's hard to stay in shape, so you end up with stiff muscles, back and neck problems, and other aches and pains.

And—I say this as a serious introvert—it's lonely. It's isolating. It can be very emotionally unhealthy when the only conversations you have for days on end are between you and the voices in your head. And they're not all that entertaining.

In my case, I haven't had a choice. My doctors have forced me to stay in bed. I've had to make the best of it, count my blessings, work around the difficulties, and be grateful for the loving support of my friends and family.

Because I see how prison-like bed rest quickly becomes, and how it can cripple other parts of my body even while it seems to heal some, I can tell you that hiding in bed is not a good thing. Not when I'm hurting physically, and not when I'm heartsick either.

Sometimes like the Victorians did, we do need to "take to our beds" for an occasional respite. It's okay now and then to stay in our pajamas and eat Double Stuf Oreos while reading novels or watching old movies.

Better yet, we can play some praise and worship music, make a cup of hot tea, wrap ourselves up in cozy quilts (crank up the air conditioning if we have to), and spend more time with Jesus.

But from experience I know that a long stint of bed rest means I'll have to spend most of the next year strengthening my muscles, dropping weight, and catching up on projects and household chores.

My point is that I would *never* choose this. I would not stay in bed if I didn't have to.

So you don't either!

Don't let the pain of your hurts and heartaches, the pain of regret, missed opportunities, poor choices, guilt, or shame imprison you. Bed may seem like a safer place, but pain will find you even there. And by hiding out, you'll only create more physical, emotional, or spiritual problems for yourself.

Don't allow yourself to grow so weak that you *can't* stand.

If you're hiding in bed as you read this, take action now. As soon as you can, begin to stretch, begin to move, begin to take small steps. Even the smallest step counts if it's a positive choice!

As the magnet on my refrigerator reads, "Do the next right thing."

If you're in such a tailspin that you can't figure out what that is, call a trusted friend or family member—someone who won't judge but will wade through the piles on the floor, sit on the end of the bed and listen, and then point out what's obvious to her and oblivious to you (and maybe kill a spider or two).

That's what I do.

Oh, and one more thing:

Just keep breathing.

CHAPTER 10

PRAYER BREATHING

Whenever I feel blue, I start breathing again.
L. FRANK BAUM

My (MARTHA'S) MOTHER used to tell me that whenever I felt stressed, I should take deep breaths in through my nose and then exhale through my mouth. This was something she would do whenever life overwhelmed her.

I tried, but it didn't work until I realized that I could mix these stress-busting breaths with another stress buster—prayer.

Prayer breathing now helps me still my racing heart and mind and silence those anxious thoughts. It works best if I focus on just a few words at a time. Most of the prayers are simple and based on Scripture.

Trying these examples may slow your heart rate, reduce stress, *and* improve your prayer life. (Who doesn't love this kind of multitasking?)

Inhale: I can
Exhale: do all
Inhale: through Christ
Exhale: my Lord.

Inhale: My God
Exhale: supplies
Inhale: my needs
Exhale: today.

Inhale: All things
Exhale: will work
Inhale: for God's
Exhale: good plan.

Inhale: Fear not,
Exhale: for you,
Inhale: my God,
Exhale: will stay
Inhale: right by
Exhale: my side
Inhale: today—
Exhale: always.

Inhale: You calmed
Exhale: the storm;
Inhale: you walked
Exhale: on waves.
Inhale: All pow'r
Exhale: is yours.

Inhale: It's you
Exhale: who saves.

Inhale: Your love
Exhale: won't fail
Inhale: when I
Exhale: am frail.
Inhale: You'll count
Exhale: my tears
Inhale: and calm
Exhale: my fears.
Inhale: Won't let
Exhale: me go.
Inhale: Won't let
Exhale: me go.

Inhale: Amaz-
Exhale: ing grace,
Inhale: how sweet
Exhale: the sound
Inhale: that saved
Exhale: a wretch like me.
Inhale: I once
Exhale: was lost,
Inhale: but now I'm found;
Exhale: was blind,
Inhale: but now
Exhale: I see.

Inhale: You love me
Exhale: unconditionally.

Inhale: You forgive me
Exhale: unreservedly.
Inhale: You redeem me
Exhale: eternally.
Inhale: You restore me
Exhale: completely.
Inhale: You renew me
Exhale: daily.
Inhale: You comfort me
Exhale: tenderly.
Inhale: You strengthen me
Exhale: mightily.
Inhale: You reign in me
Exhale: victoriously.

You can use Scripture or a favorite proverb, chorus, or hymn for prayer breathing. You can also simply speak to God from your heart.

A few words on the inhale and a few words on the exhale—that's all it takes. It's easy and healthy, and you might just see a change in your outlook!

Inhale: Breathe in;
Exhale: breathe out,
Inhale: and trust
Exhale: that God
Inhale: will be
Exhale: with you
Inhale: until
Exhale: the end
Inhale: of time.

Exhale: So breathe.
Inhale: Just breathe.
Exhale: Breathe.

Let everything that has breath praise the LORD.
Praise the LORD.

PSALM 150:6

CHAPTER 11

WEAPONS OF MASS ENCOURAGEMENT

Once you choose hope, anything's possible.
CHRISTOPHER REEVE

IF YOU WERE, for whatever nefarious reason, assigned the job of *discouraging* masses of people, where would you begin? If your goal was to dishearten the world, to convince millions of people to give in to disappointment, disillusionment, and despair, what would be your strategy?

You'd attack the encouragers first, right? You would hurt the people who have the gift of inspiration, the people who bring joy and laughter or hope and healing to others.

You'd go after the person in the family, community, or church who faithfully gives to others; who serves, mentors, supports, and nurtures.

If you can discourage the encouragers (or even better, use their pain to turn them to the dark side and make them discouragers), your work is practically done.

Of course, no one has assigned that job to you. (For the benefit of a few grumpy people we know—and some Amazon reviewers—we repeat: *No one has assigned that job to you.*)

But there is someone who has taken that mission upon himself. And you may very well be one of his targets.

The enemy of your soul would love nothing more than to *dis*courage you. He wants to *dis*able you, *dis*engage you, and *dis*mantle your hope. The battle is real, and it has bigger ramifications than your own spiritual progress.

If you're discouraged and can't encourage those within your sphere of influence, then those people will become discouraged and unable to encourage others. And on and on it goes.

Consider the opposite: If discouragement can be that powerful, then it stands to reason that unleashed encouragement could have an equal but opposite effect on the world.

If you refuse to become discouraged, then you'll lift up the people around you, who will in turn encourage the people in their world.

So fighting discouragement isn't something you do only for yourself. You fight it for all the people you care about.

I (Christin) have seen this contagious encouragement cycle happen time and again. Looking for hope in my own despair, I've shared with others something that has helped me, only to hear they've shared it with someone else, who shared it with another someone. I know my battles with discouragements have served a greater purpose!

Here's one example: I come from a large family. My parents as well as my brothers and sister and their spouses all travel and sing together. They're kind of like the von Trapps in *The Sound of Music*, only they sing best of Broadway and big band–era songs in addition to six- and eight-part a capella harmonies. In churches they also sing hymns and contemporary Christian music.

Before you ask, please take note of the message on my T-shirt: "I'm the one who doesn't sing." I'm usually in some other part of the country speaking at a women's retreat. But occasionally I join them to emcee, especially at Christmas, their busiest time of year.

They see every Christmas concert as ministry, no matter where it's scheduled or who the audience is, because people's hearts seem to be more tender at Christmas than any other time of year. The holiday brings up so many memories, so much emotion.

The state of people's hearts coupled with the clear and powerful presentation of the gospel in many of the beloved Christmas carols provide a great opportunity to touch people's lives. It's not uncommon for people to leave the concert venues beaming or teary.

Because the enemy doesn't like this kind of encouragement, all hell breaks loose for my family members as Christmas approaches each year. They nearly always get colds, coughs, or the flu, which they pass around among the thirteen of them. Their cars and vans break down, requiring costly repairs. Tires blow on the way to events. Most members of the family also have day jobs, and it's amazing how many of their bosses, clients, or customers suddenly become extremely difficult to work with at this time of year. And then the roof leaks, termites swarm, a child has a crisis at school, a church family splits, or a dear friend announces her divorce.

The hits just keep coming. The pressure builds and builds until my loved ones are all tense, distracted, frustrated, and stressed—and at one another's throats. This is not a helpful condition for doing ministry.

One year I was discouraged and depressed, particularly on their behalf. As I reviewed my prayer list, feeling totally overwhelmed by their needs, I was desperate for a shot of hope. So I started praying and reading Scripture along with encouraging words from some of my personal spiritual heroes.

As I began to feel encouraged, I knew I couldn't let the enemy keep dragging me into the pit of despair. I needed to fight back on behalf of my family. And I needed to fight *beside* them, not silently behind them.

I created a playlist of powerful worship songs declaring God's victory even in the darkest circumstances—the same ones that had ministered to me—and I made sure they took it with them on road trips.

I printed Scriptures on spiritual warfare and Scripture-based affirmations of God's love and faithfulness on poster-sized paper, and I plastered them on every flat surface in each home—on doors, cabinets, and walls. I posted them in the kitchen and laundry room—everywhere.

I sent group e-mails with words of encouragement and funny memes, including a Fred Astaire quote that's long been a family favorite. In the old musical *Finian's Rainbow*, Fred (as Finian) declares wryly, "Things are indeed hopeless. Hopeless . . . but they're not serious."

In our family, that's become code for "No matter how bad it gets, it's not the end of the world. And this is nothing in the light of eternity. We've been through worse. We'll get through this, too. We still have Jesus, and we have each other."

On a wall in my parents' house, we also posted a thankfulness tree with construction-paper leaves attached to its paper branches. Every time someone walked through the door, he or she had to write something they were thankful for on a leaf.

When I attended concerts with my family that year, I prayer-walked around the venue and let my family know what I was doing. I also asked each one for their individual prayer requests and tried to remember to send them notes or texts to remind them I was praying for them.

I won't lie: Not every member of the family is a starry-eyed optimist who embraced my efforts wholeheartedly, convinced they would make an instantaneous, supernatural difference.

That's okay. For one thing, my encouragement campaign didn't always instantaneously work. I didn't do it for praise or appreciation or even for measurable results. I did it because I believed it was the right thing to do. God had encouraged my heart, and I believed He wanted me to pass on the encouragement to my family. What they did with it—what He did with it—was out of my control.

But do you know what?

The doom-and-gloom atmosphere did lift. Family unity was restored. There was more hope, more joy, more laughter, more peace. There were still trials and tribulations all along the way, but we began to notice more blessings and answers to prayer. We were all encouraged!

And the audiences felt encouraged too.

We could hear it in the applause; we could see it in the tears streaming down their faces. The audience commented more (both in person and by e-mail) about what the music ministry had meant to them than in any previous year.

Some people were so moved after the shows or services that they couldn't talk. They just grabbed the nearest member of my family and squeezed them. Because some audience members told us, we knew they were carrying home to their families the encouragement they had received.

Of course this is just one example of many.

On smaller and larger scales, both Martha and I have witnessed the power of encouragement in numerous ways. We've seen this principle work in the lives of friends and family, too. We've seen what can happen when one person, by the grace of God, refuses to give in to discouragement and instead chooses to encourage others.

One becomes an army in no time.

The weapons of mass encouragement are powerful! Why don't you try them?

God's Word for the Weak, Worried, and Fearful

It's all too easy to feel anxious and afraid, worried, depressed, or discouraged, especially when all we can hear are negative voices: the voices of the world around us, of the enemy of our souls, or the self-defeating voices in our own heads (sometimes it's hard to tell the difference!).

At times like these, what we need is a fresh infusion of hope, a hearty helping of the Truth—straight from the source! Here are a few of our favorite verses:

> The LORD is close to the brokenhearted and saves those who are crushed in spirit. A righteous man may have many troubles, but the LORD delivers him from them all.
> PSALM 34:18-19

> I wait for the LORD, my soul waits, and in his word I put my hope.
> PSALM 130:5

You will keep in perfect peace him whose mind is steadfast, because he trusts in you.

ISAIAH 26:3

Tell fearful souls, "Courage! Take heart! GOD is here, right here, on his way to put things right and redress all wrongs. He's on his way! He'll save you!"

ISAIAH 35:4, MSG

Peace I leave with you; my peace I give you. I do not give to you as the world gives. Do not let your hearts be troubled and do not be afraid.

JOHN 14:27

I have told you these things, so that in me you may have peace. In this world you will have trouble. But take heart! I have overcome the world.

JOHN 16:33

But he said to me, "My grace is sufficient for you, for my power is made perfect in weakness." Therefore I will boast all the more gladly about my weaknesses, so that Christ's power may rest on me.

2 CORINTHIANS 12:9

That is why, for Christ's sake, I delight in weaknesses, in insults, in hardships, in persecutions, in difficulties. For when I am weak, then I am strong.

2 CORINTHIANS 12:10

Do not be anxious about anything, but in everything, by prayer and petition, with thanksgiving, present your requests to God. And the peace of God, which transcends all understanding, will guard your hearts and your minds in Christ Jesus.

PHILIPPIANS 4:6-7

I can do all things [which He has called me to do] through Him who strengthens and empowers me [to fulfill His purpose—I am self-sufficient in Christ's sufficiency; I am ready for anything and equal to anything through Him who infuses me with inner strength and confident peace.]

PHILIPPIANS 4:13, AMP

CHAPTER 12

CANDLE ON THE WATER

A mighty fortress is our God, a bulwark never failing; our helper,
He amid the flood of mortal ills prevailing.

MARTIN LUTHER

YEARS AGO, my (Christin's) father took a temporary job helping to prepare a megabookstore for its grand opening. Everything was coming together beautifully. The display shelves had been installed, and dozens of employees were hard at work unpacking boxes and boxes of books.

Suddenly, disaster struck. Someone moving a tall ladder knocked loose a sprinkler head on the ceiling, and a torrent of water gushed out of the pipe. Within seconds, the store was flooded and hundreds of books were destroyed. It was a colossal mess.

What do you think the employees did at that moment?

Did they burst into tears? Wring their hands helplessly? Stand around yelling at the ladder mover? Quit and walk out because they were frustrated and discouraged? Did they run home to climb in bed and pull the covers over their heads?

Not hardly.

One person quickly called the authorities so the water main would be turned off. My dad quickly scaled the ladder, jammed two or three of his fingers into the pipe, and closed his other hand over it to stem the flow of water. Most of the water then ran down his arms and soaked him instead of spraying wildly all over the store.

As Dad held his position on the ladder, everyone else rushed to move all the boxes and shelves far away from the damaged sprinkler head to save as many books as they could. And because they took action, all was *not* lost.

The damage was much less than it could have been. The store was even able to open on time.

Sometimes I can't help but think of that story when I look around at our world today. It's an even bigger mess than a bookstore under water.

I'll be honest: There are times when the troubles of the world so overwhelm me that I want to walk away. Make that run away—to take cover in the nearest pillowy spot and pretend I haven't seen anything.

If friends happen to be nearby as I hear the day's latest tragedy, I catch their eyes, and we often find ourselves shaking our heads and sighing and wringing our hands helplessly. It can quickly turn into the saddest pajama party ever as we all peek out from our respective covers just long enough to talk about the latest crisis we've discovered via Facebook or Twitter and wonder aloud how it will impact future generations of our families and society as a whole.

Thankfully, after a minute or two, we usually remember (or

try to remind each other, anyway) that we can't give in to discouragement or give up in despair. We do not live (or grieve) as those "who have no hope" (1 Thessalonians 4:13).

So how *do* we live? What do we do when we don't know what to do?

Scripture says to "make the most of every opportunity" (Colossians 4:5) and to "live holy and godly lives as you look forward to the day of God and speed its coming" (2 Peter 3:11-12).

The answer is not to sit atop our mattresses and wait while the floodwaters rise.

We're called to be a light—a lighthouse, if you will—to those lost in the storm. We have to get busy reaching out to others; there are so many who have yet to hear the Good News of the gospel—those who have no hope.

Even in our own struggles, we can still offer comfort to others enduring pain and suffering or to those who have been rejected or overlooked. Sometimes especially *because* of our struggles, we are uniquely qualified.

My friend Jennifer, who lost six babies to miscarriage and stillbirth before conceiving twins, writes a blog and hosts Bible studies for other women who are waiting on God, undergoing infertility treatment, or grieving loss.

Another woman I know handwrites beautiful notes of encouragement to others while she undergoes chemotherapy treatments for a rare genetic disorder.

Gene, who moved many times during his military service, spends every Saturday building homes for people in need so they can have the security of owning the roof over their heads.

Lois, single and in her fifties, let her loneliness motivate her to reach out to others in need of community. She stood in line *voluntarily* at the Department of Motor Vehicles (hard to believe,

I know) so she could be licensed to drive the church bus on Sundays. Now she transports the congregation's elderly widows, who would otherwise be stuck at home.

While battling her own cancer, Martha's sister Melva asked her daughter to drive her around looking for homeless women who were about her size so she could give her clothes to them. She knew the healing power of giving to others in the midst of your own need. Melva had always been the type of person who would give the shirt off her back to anyone in need. Why, she must have figured, should she allow cancer to keep her from continuing to do that?

None of us is as helpless as we sometimes feel.

Even when our world is falling apart, we *can* make a difference. We can still stand for God's truth, love, and grace. We can take some kind of action. We can give, love, serve, and pray. It doesn't have to be a Herculean effort: "Little is much when God is in it" (see Matthew 14:17-21).

I don't have many memories of my great-grandmother on my mother's side since she died when I was very young. But I know she was a traveling evangelist in her senior years and that she greatly and positively influenced generations of our family and those she ministered to. One of the first children's hymns I learned was a favorite of hers:

Jesus bids us shine,
With a pure, clear light,
Like a little candle,
Burning in the night.
In this world is darkness,
So let us shine—
You in your small corner,
And I in mine.[4]

Her daughter (my grandmother), now 104 and blind with glaucoma, still sits in her rocking chair in the nursing home every day, praying for each of her many family members by name while knitting scarves for the homeless.

Whether we're closing off a burst water pipe, lighting a candle, feeding the hungry, comforting the lonely, clothing the needy, or leading the lost to Jesus, we can each do something that will make a difference to someone. We can brighten our own little corners and together light our world.

> In the same way, let your light shine before men, that
> they may see your good deeds and praise your Father
> in heaven.
>
> MATTHEW 5:16

CHAPTER 13

WHENEVER YOU'RE READY

In part one we've shared a few of our fears and worries. We know that facing difficult emotions isn't easy and that sometimes you *do* need to rest in the arms of Jesus. But there comes a time to take a deep breath, put on your "big girl" pants, and face the fear head on. It may be the only way a situation is ever going to improve. We hope this chapter gives you the encouragement you need to face your feelings (when you'd rather hide).

Letting in the Light

Take time to reflect on the following questions. You might want to jot down your answers in a separate notebook (or on the back of a magazine or take-out menu or paper bag—whatever's within easy reach).

1. How much would you say fear is a factor in your life right now? How often is it something you battle?

    ___ Once in a while

    ___ Fairly frequently

    ___ Almost constantly

    ___ I'm diving for the cover(s)

    ___ I'm reading this from a bunker

2. When have your fears been unfounded? When have you worried or agonized over something that never happened?

3. When has a healthy apprehension helped you?

4. What happened when your fears were realized? What was that like?

5. When has God helped you overcome your fears? What has facing fear in the past taught you? Can you apply that lesson now?

Scriptures for Meditation

Be strong and courageous. Do not be afraid or terrified because of them, for the LORD your God goes with you; he will never leave you nor forsake you.

DEUTERONOMY 31:6

The LORD is my light and my salvation—whom shall I fear? The LORD is the stronghold of my life—of whom shall I be afraid? . . . I am still confident of this: I will see the goodness of the LORD in the land of the living.

PSALM 27:1, 13

Because you are my help, I sing in the shadow of your
wings. My soul clings to you; your right hand upholds me.
PSALM 63:7-8

Immediately he [Jesus] spoke to them and said, "Take
courage! It is I. Don't be afraid."
MARK 6:50

God did not give us a spirit of timidity, but a spirit of
power, of love and of self-discipline.
2 TIMOTHY 1:7

Humble yourselves, therefore, under God's mighty hand,
that he may lift you up in due time. Cast all your anxiety
on him because he cares for you.
1 PETER 5:6-7

Pushing Back the Covers

Time to think about moving!

Read the Scriptures for meditation and ask yourself what God
might be saying to your heart. Copy the verses or other inspirational words and phrases on sticky notes and put them on your
headboard, nightstand, bathroom mirror, or anywhere you'll
notice them throughout your day.

You can also find free online meme generators that will help
you make Scripture graphics to use as wallpaper for your phone,
tablet, or computer.

Here's another great way to surround yourself with courage-
building and faith-affirming Scripture: Certain companies
will embroider or silk-screen your favorite verses onto your

pillowcases. That way you can read them before you fall asleep at night and the first thing in the morning.

Or download one of the many free audio versions of Scripture (or if you're old school as we sometimes are, pull out your Scripture CDs or cassettes!) and listen as you fall asleep. We know people who play the Scriptures at a low volume all night long. They like that they're filling their subconscious minds with God's Word, and whenever they wake up in the night, it's the first thing they hear.

Feet on the Floor

Try these first steps:

Write a letter to yourself filled with encouraging comments you would love to hear from others.

Think of one positive step (for yourself, your family, your career or ministry) that you are delaying because you're fearful. Then take that step!

Make a list of ten or fifteen activities you enjoy and simple everyday actions that make you happy. Keep them handy for the next time you feel discouraged and need a lift. Here are a few of ours:

1. Encourage some people, even if you don't think they need it. They usually do.
2. Write or call a friend just to say hello and catch up.
3. Meet a deadline.
4. Throw away at least twenty pieces of paper every day to help declutter your life, or a higher number if you are on a roll.
5. Read a good book.

6. Send someone a thank-you note for a gift or a thoughtful gesture. Better yet, write a legacy thank-you—letting someone know of the lasting impact he or she has made on your life.

7. Try one of the awesome recipes or craft projects you pinned on Pinterest.

8. Let your dog take you for a walk and share a latte.

9. Listen to a favorite podcast.

10. Host a brunch, lunch, or pajama party and have real conversation with good friends.

11. Find a new adventure to have within five miles of your house.

12. Organize something—a closet, a drawer, a folder on your computer—that you've been putting off, or help someone else with an organization project.

13. Plan a grown-up scavenger hunt (google this term for ideas) in your neighborhood or community.

14. Take photographs of beautiful, funny, or unusual things you've never noticed before. Spread the joy with others (on social media, for instance), or just savor them yourself.

15. Pass along a kindness that someone once showed to you. Pay it forward.

Every day, try to do *one* thing that helps you overcome fear and inertia, makes you happier and healthier, or blesses someone else's life.

PART TWO

Facing People When You'd Rather Run

I never leaf through a copy of National Geographic *without realizing how lucky we are to live in a society where it is traditional to wear clothes.*
ERMA BOMBECK

BEING MEMBERS OF THE HUMAN RACE means we all make mistakes. (Mullets and mom jeans come to mind.)

We fail to do or say what we should do or say; we hurt others without realizing it. We're sure you can think of examples in your own life! We can, because like you (and everyone else), we're not perfect. The regret and embarrassment make us want to run and hide.

And when other imperfect people wound us; when they reject, abandon, or betray us; when they don't live up to our expectations; or when they ignore their own imperfections, what are we inclined to do?

Retreat. Hide somewhere safe where we won't have to face those people ever again.

We go pillow diving.

But we're here to remind you (and ourselves) that there are good reasons to come out from under the comforter. For one thing, there's freedom in learning to stand up and accept responsibility for yourself and your own peace. There's also freedom in learning to set healthy boundaries and in learning to forgive. And when you decide to stop hiding from people, the blessings and rewards of personal growth and maturity, healing, and restoration will follow. We don't want you to miss these perks, so read on!

CHAPTER 14

SKINNY GENES

Sand irritates the oyster, and the oyster responds by forming
a beautiful pearl.
ANONYMOUS

I HEAR NEARLY EVERY family has one. There's always an irritat-
ingly, inexplicably thin person who crushes your theory of why
you weigh what you do. If this relative exists, how can you possibly have an uncontrollable, inherited weight condition that
provides an excuse to abstain from dieting?

In our family, this person is my younger sister: a bubbly,
blonde-haired, blue-eyed slip of a girl. While the rest of us are
miserably counting calories and toting up exchanges, chewing
on celery and rice cakes, or wracked with guilt over the cheese-
cake we accidentally inhaled last night in a moment of weakness,
she's distraught that her doctor says she needs to put on a few
pounds.

"You all have no idea how hard it is for me!" she wails.

She's right. We don't.

"I'm so full," she complains, after taking two bites of each of the six entrées she's ordered for dinner. We'd slap her, but we're too busy divvying up the leftovers.

"I've got dibs on the prime rib! Could somebody pass me the alfredo?"

I guess she does feel a little left out at family functions, when we're all comparing our weight-loss woes. She can't contribute anything to a conversation on the pros and cons of the South Beach Diet or Weight Watchers vs. Jenny Craig.

After last year's Fourth of July picnic, she cornered me in the kitchen.

"I'm not that skinny," she insisted. "Look at my tummy. See?!"

She pulled up her shirt and proudly pointed to her "protruding" abdomen.

"Those are your internal organs," I said.

Against my better judgment, I once agreed to accompany her as she shopped for clothes. I waited outside the dressing room for hours. When everything fits you, how hard can it be to find something? It's not as if she's in there trying to squeeze size sixteen hips into size twelve "stretch" jeans. Now that can be painful *and* time-consuming.

After what seemed like an eternity, she finally emerged with a quizzical expression on her face. "I don't know which ones to get," she said, holding up two equally tiny pairs of jeans that looked like they'd be big on Barbie. "I can fit in the size zero, but I think the size one looks better. What do you think I should do?"

Several suggestions came to mind, but none that I could repeat in public—or here. After a few moments of stony silence, I managed to mutter, "I feel your pain," as I propelled her full force toward the cash register.

Family—can't live with 'em, can't live without 'em.

No one else knows quite so well how to push our buttons, irritate and upset us, or do a happy dance on our very last nerve. When we're close, no one is closer, but when something drives us apart? No wounds are quite so deep.

Those wounds can be so painful we might be tempted to dive under the duvet and stay there, hiding from our families and the trauma and drama they trigger.

Some of us express our feelings in a torrent of tears or a terrific tantrum; others have perfected stony silence. Maybe we're the ones on the receiving end of that tantrum or silence. Either way, it's a pretty uncomfortable bed we're lying on.

We can grow a lot of chin hair waiting for family members to apologize and see our point of view. It's just not pretty.

Thankfully, not all relationships are toxic. Some just need a little repairing now and then. We may need to make the first move—to take responsibility for our part in the situation, to do what we can to reopen lines of communication and participate in the restoration process. We may need to forgive without first receiving an apology.

Sometimes we may not only need to forgive a relative but also set healthier boundaries, especially in toxic relationships. In certain situations, we may even need to take a step back and limit our time with family members who aren't interested in or willing to work with us toward healthier relationships. We can still love, pray for, and forgive others without exposing ourselves to further hurt. We can move on with our own lives today while keeping our hearts open to the possibility of change, growth, healing, and/or reconciliation in the future.

If you're struggling with nonskinny genes or other family issues, don't forget about Colossians 3:12-14:

As God's chosen people, holy and dearly loved, clothe yourselves with compassion, kindness, humility, gentleness and patience. Bear with each other and forgive . . . as the Lord forgave you. And over all these virtues put on love, which binds them all together in perfect unity.

Love is a much better look on everyone! It's unquestionably a better choice than squeezing into those skinny jeans.

So let's love, give, and forgive for Jesus' sake, doing what we can to make things right and live at peace "as far as it depends on" us (Romans 12:18).

CHAPTER 15

WHAT KIND OF FOOL AM I?

I discovered an astonishing truth: God is attracted to weakness. He cannot resist those who humbly and honestly admit how desperately they need him.
JIM CYMBALA

HAVE YOU EVER BEEN so embarrassed by something you did or didn't do—that you felt like you could never show your face again?

Some of us may not like to admit it, but we all have those experiences: memories of times we hurt others or disappointed them, or they believe we did. Somehow, we failed to meet their needs, standards, or expectations, both realistic and unrealistic. Frankly, we've also failed to meet our own standards or expectations, both realistic and unrealistic.

It's a blow to our pride. It shatters our ego. We feel miserable and worthless; we don't ever want to get out of bed again.

But lying there, repeatedly reliving every embarrassing moment, every humiliating experience, and every disappointment won't improve anything.

We may not be able to fix the mistakes, gaffes, and crippling fears of the past, either long ago or yesterday. But we have control over what we choose to do with *this day*, today.

The way forward starts with this simple realization:

You are more than the mistakes, oversights, and surrenders you have made.

You are more than your mistakes. They don't define you. They don't confine you. You can learn to let them go and leave them behind you.

Think about it: The Bible is chock-full of messed-up, mixed-up people who were forgiven, redeemed, and restored by God. These people's humiliating stumbles and falls from grace have been permanently memorialized in the pages of Scripture for generations to read and remember.

Abraham was a coward. Jacob was a liar. Moses was a hothead. Rahab was a prostitute. David was an adulterer. Jonah was a whiner and a runner from God. Matthew was a cheater. Martha was a busybody. Thomas was a doubter. Prior to his conversion, the apostle Paul was a Pharisee who killed Christians in the name of God.

These men and women had serious character flaws! They made major mistakes. They were all too human. But God worked in them and through them to accomplish great and mighty things for His Kingdom.

In 2 Corinthians 4:7, Paul explains, "We have this treasure in jars of clay to show that this all-surpassing power is from God and not from us."

He goes on to say, "Therefore I will boast all the more gladly about my weaknesses, so that Christ's power may rest on me. That is why, for Christ's sake, I delight in weaknesses, in insults, in hardships, in persecutions, in difficulties. For when I am weak, then I am strong" (2 Corinthians 12:9-10).

Wait . . . *what?* Boasting in our weaknesses? Not tucking them deep between the covers? We're supposed to boast about— our "trip over our shoelaces, sitting in the back rows, hanging our heads down" kind of weaknesses? That's what we're to gladly talk about? That mistake, that blunder, that procrastination, that apathy? That timidity? Seriously? Are we to *delight* in them as Paul did?

Yes! Because that's how the world can see Jesus in us. In our weaknesses, God's power and strength are revealed. Through the cracks in our broken, messed-up lives, His light shines brightly.

We don't need to be perfect or pious or put together. We don't need to match up to what others think we should be. What we need to do is allow God to heal us, restore us, and grow us in His grace. We need to be willing and available to let Him do His work in us and through us—even in our brokenness.

> Brothers, I do not consider myself yet to have taken hold of it. But one thing I do: Forgetting what is behind and straining toward what is ahead, I press on toward the goal to win the prize for which God has called me heavenward in Christ Jesus.
>
> PHILIPPIANS 3:13-14

Each and every day, God uses ordinary people like us to do extraordinary things for Him. We regularly hear their stories in church or on YouTube or Facebook, or we find them in the inspirational section of the bookstore. People in our communities and in our own families meet this description.

One of these days, you could meet this description!

You just have to be willing to push back the covers and get out of bed.

Nothing is too hard for God, no sin too difficult for His love to overcome, no failure that He cannot make into a success.[1]

OSWALD CHAMBERS

Top Ten Things You *Wish* Someone Would Say to the Bedridden

10. Move over. I've brought chocolate!
9. I passed all the dishes and laundry on my way in. Did you hear there's a new app for that?
8. Want me to fluff your pillow for you? And look, I've brought four more!
7. Hey, I found the remote—and your other sock!
6. Do you need anything? Books, magazines, a Caribbean cruise?
5. Don't worry, I would *never* tag you. Plus I know how to Photoshop.
4. I care.
3. I can't imagine the pain you're going through, but I'm here for you.
2. I honestly don't know what you need, but here's something I can do.
1. You know, there was a time when I had the covers pulled over my head, and I didn't think I'd ever get out of bed. But eventually the day came when I was ready to face the world again. It will come for you, too.

CHAPTER 16

WHEN BOUNDARIES DON'T ABOUND

We must not confuse the command to love with the disease to please.
LYSA TERKEURST

THE DICTIONARY DEFINES a boundary as something that marks a limit. Personal boundaries define who we are and who we are not, what we are willing and not willing to do—and what kind of behavior we will or will not tolerate from others.

Sometimes we don't have appropriate personal boundaries; sometimes we do, and other people cross them. Henry Cloud, author of *Boundaries,* says these personal limits are actually a litmus test for the quality of our relationship.

"Those people in our lives who can respect our boundaries will love our wills, our opinions, our separateness," he writes. "Those who can't respect our boundaries are telling us that they don't love our 'no.' They only love our 'yes,' our compliance."[2]

Sometimes we're so intent on being helpful that we mistakenly cross other people's boundaries.

Once, when I (Martha) was walking toward the entrance door of a restaurant, I saw an elderly man attempting to exit the restaurant while balancing himself on his walker. I was trying to get to the door to help him, but when I pulled the door open from my side, he reached for it at that exact moment. When the door flung open he had nothing to hold onto, and he almost tumbled to the ground in front of me. I was embarrassed and profusely apologized. I was sorry that my desire to be kind almost made the man fall flat on his face!

A desire to be kind also can lead us into trouble with our own boundaries. We may think we're being deferential or polite, when in reality we're inviting people to stomp all over our limits (if we have any). For example, we can do this by avoiding conflict or confrontation. We may bite our tongue and refrain from saying what we need to say to a certain person. Then we become upset, frustrated, or angry when that person walks all over us or keeps behaving in ways that hurt us.

We can both share about times when speaking up has literally saved our lives or the lives of those we've loved. Even though it wasn't easy, even though our insides were in a knot, and even though we didn't want to rock the boat, we finally summoned the courage to do it: to draw a line in the sand, to defend the defenseless, to put an end to bullying, to say enough is enough, to require more of someone, and to make a stand.

Once when I was in the hospital, the nurse came into my room and told me that I needed more insulin. At that moment, I was feeling dizzy, sweaty, clammy, and shaky—all signs that my blood sugar had dropped too low. I didn't think I needed the extra insulin, because it would have made my blood sugar drop even lower!

Appearing not to appreciate my questioning her judgment,

the nurse said I did in fact need the insulin. I decided to let her have her way, but then, as she prepared the shot, something inside me kept warning me to speak up. It wasn't audible. But it was a clear directive that made my heart pound, even more than it was doing from the low blood sugar.

Finally, just as she was swabbing my upper arm with rubbing alcohol in preparation for giving me another dose of insulin, I spoke up.

The nurse was holding the needle at my arm, ready to plunge it in, when I managed to get the words out.

"Um, I, um, really don't think I, um . . . need that."

"Yes, you do," she said.

Well, I tried, I told myself. And I almost gave in. She was so authoritative. But my racing heart wouldn't let me.

"Could you test my blood first, before you give it?"

She wasn't very happy but agreed to do so. The blood test would give a more current reading and thus be more accurate.

The nurse left the room and ordered the blood test, and I waited for the results. I sat alone in my room, still shaky and dizzy, and now wondering if I had done the right thing.

After about twenty minutes, several nurses came rushing into my room with orange juice. My blood sugar reading had turned out to be dangerously below normal.

Speaking up had indeed been the right thing to do. In fact, the nurse on duty later that evening, after having read my chart, told me that if the first nurse had given me the shot, I likely would have gone into a coma and not seen morning.

I thanked God that day, and many days since, for the courage He gave me to speak up at that right moment. Silence isn't always the best policy.

Conflict avoidance often fools us into thinking it is the

peaceful solution to our problems. But it can leave us with more problems and pain than an actual heart-to-heart talk with the person we are avoiding, especially if that person is willing to be respectful, consider the facts, and take responsibility for his or her own role in the matter.

It reminds us of the oft-quoted story of the mother who woke up her son one morning and told him it was time to go to church. He pulled the covers tighter over his head and flatly refused.

When she insisted, he replied, "I'm not going, and I'll tell you why. They don't like me there, and I don't like them."

"You will go," his mother answered, "and I'll tell *you* why. You're the pastor."

Most of us don't want to have to challenge, correct, confront, or speak the truth in love.

Let the bossies, bullies, and bad guys have their way; we'll take it all lying down. Hiding under the covers, curled up in a fetal position, we hope that those who seek our harm or want to sidetrack us from what God has given us to do will grow tired and go away.

We'll play dead, like they tell you to do when a grizzly bear is breathing down your neck. Except grizzly bears don't always go away. Sometimes they want to flex their muscles and remind us that we are no match for their ferocity. They see us standing in the way of their berries, and they are more than happy to snap us in two, like twigs.

We think we're better off staying in our tents, turning out our flashlights, and not making any sounds. Yet that action, or inaction, doesn't do us or anyone else any good. We can't hide forever. We have to eat, too, just like the bear. There are people who depend on us, just as the bear has cubs that depend on her.

But unlike the bear, we can't take the winter off, don't have night vision, and don't weigh more than a thousand pounds. We're only human.

We have a Father who wants the best for us, who knows the natural abilities He created in us. But sometimes we're cowering in so much fear, regret, or feelings of inadequacy or inferiority that we forget that truth.

Frozen is a Disney movie; it shouldn't be our battle plan.

The healthy boundaries God calls us to develop and maintain go far beyond the presumed safety of our tents or corners of our beds! He wants us to have and respect healthy boundaries, whether they are ours or someone else's, so we can effectively accomplish His plan for our lives.

Top Ten Reasons to Find Your Spine—and Use It!

10. You'll save a fortune in chiropractor bills.
9. You'll look like you've lost fifteen pounds overnight with your new posture!
8. You'll find all kinds of things you thought were lost forever on the upper bookshelves and countertops in your home.
7. Your clothes will fit better.
6. Your head will have something to rest on.
5. You'll no longer be marketed as the world's most absorbent doormat.
4. Others will have to look you in the eye. (They earn a free pass if your head is always down.)
3. You'll gain muscle, coordination, strength—and self-respect.
2. You'll be able to see your way forward.
1. You will walk confidently into your future.

CHAPTER 17

IF YOU NEED ME, I'LL BE SLEEPING OVER THERE

The dearest friend on earth is a mere shadow compared with Jesus Christ.
OSWALD CHAMBERS

THE BIBLE TELLS US that after Jesus was taken by the Roman soldiers while He and His disciples were in a place called Gethsemane, He was brought before Caiaphas, the high priest. The teachers of the law and the elders had assembled to discuss what they would do with Jesus. In actuality, their plan was already in place.

Matthew 26:58 says that Peter, one of the disciples and a close friend of Jesus, followed Jesus at a distance, right to the courtyard of the high priest. Peter entered and sat down with the guards, probably in the back, to "see the outcome."

If you've ever experienced a crisis and felt abandoned by some of those "close friends" who simply "followed at a distance," who may have "sat down" with those who were carrying out an injustice, waiting safely on the sidelines to "see the outcome" so they could decide which side to be on, then you know how Jesus was feeling that day. He knew His suffering was in God's redemptive plan and for an eternal good, but it still had to hurt and disappoint Him to see the actions, or inactions, of those He had called His friends.

Take Peter, for example. At the Last Supper when Jesus predicted that His disciples would "fall away" when the time of His death came, Peter was first to deflect Jesus' words.

"The others may desert you, Jesus, but me? Peter? Never!" he said. (This is a bit paraphrased, but you get the gist.)

It was a dramatic delivery of, at least for the moment, a heartfelt pledge. Perhaps the scene continued something like this, at least in today's vernacular:

"Me? *Me,* Jesus? This is Peter you're talking to! You told me to come to You on the water. And I did. Remember? Okay, I took my eyes off of You, but only for a moment, and that's when I started to sink and You had to save me. But I still went out there, Jesus. I took some steps on that water. Several, as a matter of fact. Maybe more. And where were the rest of the guys? That's right—still in the boat! I was the only one to step out when You said 'Come.' That should tell you how loyal I am to you. Deny you? Never!"

Peter was emphatic, and almost insulted at the mere thought that he would betray his friend.

Has a friend ever pledged that kind of allegiance to you with that kind of passion? Maybe she said something similar to this:

"You are my BFF. My best friend forever! You're the most incredible person I know. Where would I be without you? I could never repay you for all you've done for me."

And then, the storm, a test, false accusations, or misunderstandings come, and this friend hides out in the shadows.

Like Peter, she sits safely "at a distance," watching and listening in on the ill-willed conversations.

Peter, who had seen Jesus walking on water, would deny Him three times.

And now the chief priests and all the Sanhedrin press the crowd for testimony that they can use against Jesus, so they can put Him to death. But nothing sticks, even though plenty of false witnesses step forward.

Still, Peter watches in silence. He could have spoken up in Jesus' defense, but he didn't. No doubt there was too much noise going on in his head:

I know I fell asleep in the garden when you asked us to stay awake and watch while you prayed, Jesus, but James and John fell asleep too. Maybe it was all that bread we ate.

But when they captured you in the garden, didn't I stand up for you against the high priest's servant? I cut his ear right off! You saw it yourself. Still not sure why You went and put it back on the man, healing him right there on the spot. But that was Your call. You do that a lot. They're trying to hurt You, and You're kind to them. I'll never understand that about You. Maybe you want to handle this Your own way.

Peter listens awhile "at a distance" and chooses not to become involved.

All You have to do is give the word, Jesus, and we'll all stand up for You. I don't know where everyone else is, but they're probably around here somewhere. We'll do it, Jesus. We're here. We've got Your back; we're just not letting anyone know it right now. You understand. We're incognito friends—at your service, at a distance.

Silence. That's all Jesus gets from all of His friends. Even Peter sits on the bench with the guards, in the shadows, waiting to see the outcome.

Meanwhile, in real time, the waves of accusations rise higher and higher around Jesus.

Why isn't He calming this storm? Peter wonders. *If You could walk on water, You could walk right out of here, untouched.*

Jesus remains silent. And so does Peter. The "Surely not me" disciple doesn't speak a word aloud in his friend's defense. The disciple who was so full of confidence and bravado only hours ago, if that, now watches.

This time, he doesn't long to walk out to Him. Not in this kind of a storm.

Peter is fearful. If he steps out of his silence, will Jesus save him this time? *Can* He save him this time? Surely, if Jesus could walk on water—Peter had seen it firsthand. Still, this is an angry mob. And yes, Peter had seen his Lord heal the blind and even raise the dead. But this? Look at all the people plotting against Him and calling for His death. They could just as easily turn on Peter, too. What was he supposed to do now?

He could have done *something, anything* to help his friend. But faithful, devoted, steadfast, impulsive Peter remains silent, watching his friend from afar.

Peter doesn't speak up until he's asked if he knows Him. Then the one who had pledged to never deny his friend flatly denies Him. Driven by fear, confusion, self-interest, self-preservation, or whatever—he abandons Jesus.

Whatever you're going through, however abandoned you feel, however long you've prayed for the hurt of the betrayal to stop or for someone to stand up in your defense, be assured that Jesus understands the pain you're feeling!

He cares about your broken heart.

He's a friend who won't remain silent or watch from a distance, waiting to see the outcome before becoming involved. He has promised to stand by your side in every situation. He will be your advocate.

He died on the cross to prove His love for you, to prove His friendship.

Jesus never sleeps, so He won't leave you on your worst day or when you're facing your greatest challenge. He's a faithful friend. He loves you, and He doesn't care who knows it!

And He'll always have your back, even when you don't have His.

Be Your Own Best Friend

Whoever . . .

    hurt you
    left you
    refused to accept you
    overlooked your need
    discounted your worth
    lied to you or about you
    didn't see your pain
    bullied you
    laughed at you
    abandoned you
    betrayed you

broke you

devastated you

convinced you that you'd never be any more than the person they want you to be for their own reasons (usually to feel better about themselves) . . .

Don't let them win.

They may have labeled you, but their label is far from accurate.

They may have attacked you, ridiculed you, treated you like you're worthless, or made you want to run away and hide. But don't fall in with their plans for you. Move on with your life. You have better things to do.

Even if *you* are the loudest negative voice in your own head, stop listening! Maybe you hear yourself asking,

Who do you think you are?

Whatever made you think you could accomplish that?

You're nothing but a failure.

You don't do anything right.

You'll never get your act together.

If only you had . . .

If only you were . . .

If only you could . . .

If those are the words tumbling around in your head, answer yourself as though you're talking to a friend you truly care about. You've let the negative voices take center stage in your life long enough. Replace them with voices of truth.

You are loved by God.

You have value.

Your life is worth living.

You are accepted.

Don't let anyone, any hurt, or anything else convince you otherwise!

If no one else is speaking up for you, speak up for yourself. Be your own counselor, your own cheerleader, your own best friend.

Do something else for yourself: Seek help as soon as you can. Talk to a boss, teacher, pastor, parent, spouse, or friend.

Sometimes it's hard to ask, but everyone needs help sometimes.

Life can get tough. People can be mean. Maybe a family member or a friend has betrayed or hurt you. Maybe a supervisor or coworker has made your life unbelievably difficult. These people have made your challenges harder and your journey more treacherous than it needed to be. You might even find yourself so injured that you have become numb, and now you are desperately trying to feel something—anything—again.

This isn't the day, the way, or the place for your hope to end. It's not in the plan. What plan, you may ask?

The one God has for you!

He created you with a clear plan in mind. No matter what has happened in your life, His plan hasn't changed.

Your life is meant to go on until you've seen all you are meant to see, gone everywhere you are meant to go, and accomplished everything you were born to do.

A bully can't stop that.

Discouragement can't either.

No obstacle that someone tries to throw in your path can truly block what God has intended for you.

After my (Martha's) first humorous opinion piece was published, an anonymous person sent a letter to the editor. The letter's author said I had no business writing anything ever again. I cried when I read it, shook in fear of future criticism throughout the night, and contemplated following his advice and giving up writing forever.

Then, I took a deep breath and went on with my life.

That humorous opinion piece turned into a nine-year newspaper column. Now, eighty-eight books, dozens of plays, and an Emmy nomination later, I'm glad I didn't let his hurtful words stop God's plan for my life.

I later discovered that a middle-school boy, who was no doubt doing a class assignment to write a letter to the editor, wrote that letter! He probably had to choose something to write about and was annoyed when he couldn't grasp the satire of my piece. He had no idea how hurtful to me his careless words had been.

Some people aren't truly bullies as much as pests: those rude, irritating, insensitive people God might use as grains of sand to irritate us just enough to produce pearls of wisdom and maturity!

If you are dealing with a bona fide bully, it can be helpful to remember a few things.

Some bullies are driven by insecurity and jealousy. Something is missing in their own lives. They're envious of who you are, or of something you're doing or achieving. Without even realizing it, you might represent something they wish they had.

Others exhibit a form of mental illness that keeps them from experiencing genuine emotion; they enjoy provoking other people. It amuses them to see people in pain, and they're incapable of feeling empathy. If you spend time online, you know there's a name for these people: trolls. Do you also know there's a method for dealing with them? Here it is: Don't feed them!

Don't give them the reaction or response they're looking for.

Don't change who you are to make these people feel better about themselves. You aren't the problem.

They may try to rob you of the joy you find in your life, your work, and your loved ones. Don't let them.

And remember, your encouragement might not come from the people you expect it to come from. It hurts when it doesn't, but

God may, and often does, send encouragement through someone else. Sometimes that needed boost comes from a complete stranger.

My (Martha's) grandson, Kyle Bolton, had been bullied in his last school and beaten up twice—once in the hallway and once when he was followed into the boys' restroom. None of us would have even known about that last incident had a mother not intercepted the cell phone video that was being passed around at a school basketball game. She turned it in to the principal, and the school suspended the students responsible for the severe bullying for six months.

But my grandson was now attending a different school, with different kids. Yet it was happening again, and the story felt all too familiar.

It started with kids throwing pencils and pens at him, and then thick balls of paper. This time, though, instead of waiting until things escalated, he went straight to the principal's office after class. He told her what had happened at his previous school. The principal was concerned, and so was a member of the school's football team who happened to be helping out in the principal's office that day and overheard the conversation.

After my grandson left the principal's office, the football player caught up with him in the hallway.

"What class did this happen in?" the football player asked.

When my grandson told him, this thoughtful student said he would stop by.

Sure enough, the next day as my grandson was doing his work, he noticed his teacher talking to someone at the door. The next thing he knew, this football player walked into the classroom— and so did the entire school football team! The players lined up on either side of the room, and then that first player stepped to the front of the class. He warned the students that anyone even *thinking* about bullying my grandson would have to go through not only him but also the whole football team! Then he began to point to other kids in the classroom, saying, "Or if you're thinking about bullying her, or him, or him, you're going to have to go through all of us. We've got their backs!"

My grandson was overwhelmed. He told me all he could do the rest of the day was smile—on the outside and the inside. In the days, weeks, and even months that followed, whenever he passed certain members of the football team, they'd stop and ask how he was doing.

That moment is one our grandson will never forget. He had found the courage to stand up for himself, and someone else decided to stand with him, be a friend, and change his life forever.

So take a deep breath. If you're being harassed, mistreated, or bullied, it may be hard to see your future right now, especially if someone is making you feel like you have none. It's hard to see your worth when friends have betrayed you, a husband or boyfriend has left you, or people you thought would stand up for you didn't. But none of that changes your worth. How people treat you doesn't change your value.

And what about the bully? Leave room for people to grow. Whoever hurt you could have a change of heart (yes, miracles do happen) and apologize to you someday. But if he or she doesn't do that, you can still move past the hurt.

To do that, you may have to take another step away from your bed, stand up for yourself, and ask for help just as my grandson did. You *can* grow strong enough to stand in spite of any bully in your life. And you *can* become strong enough to continue standing. All it takes is practice and the right kind of friends around you. They're out there, just waiting to meet you. But you'll have to leave your bed to find them.

CHAPTER 18

NONE OF THIS IS EASY

God says we need to love our enemies. It hard to do. But it can start by telling the truth.

AIBILEEN CLARK, in *The Help (film version)*

ONCE, WHILE DRIVING DOWN A HIGHWAY, my (Martha's) husband and I were having a discussion about some people we needed to forgive. We felt as if they had ripped out our hearts and kicked them to the curb. Forgiveness was difficult to think about, much less offer.

So we continued privately processing the pain together, which, by the way, is a perfectly healthy thing to do. Not so healthy is when you're "processing" it on Facebook, or in "anonymous" comments, or by hiring a skywriting airplane to list your grievances so all the world can see. According to my Bible, that's not quite the type of forgiveness Jesus spoke about.

The pain we were feeling was raw and hurt deeply, and it was just too hard to forgive in that moment.

My husband had to pull over to the side of the road for a

minute, and we were still talking about our feelings while parked there. When we were ready to pull back onto the road, I noticed that we had been parked under a billboard. It was similar to one of those "Signed, God" billboards that you sometimes see. You know the ones I'm talking about:

Just saying hello.

—God

How long was I supposed to stay on hold? You called Me when you almost hit that car, but after it was safe, you never came back on the line. You still there?

—God

This billboard, the one we had parked under, displayed only two words:

Forgive them.

Just two words on a billboard that we *happened* to park under on a day when we really didn't feel like forgiving "them."

A word from God? Yeah, I'd say so. Chances are it had been there for months, maybe even years. But it was also there on that particular day, at that particular hour, the very minute we needed it.

This forgiveness thing is hard, isn't it? So hard that it may have been what Jesus was sweating blood over in the garden of Gethsemane. Maybe His impending death wasn't what was playing over and over in His head. Perhaps it was the visual of Him hanging on that cross, knowing He would have to look at those people, the ones who had falsely accused Him, who had scourged

Him, mocked Him, pierced His hands and feet, and left Him to die. He would have to look them in the eye and forgive them!

That would make you sweat drops of blood, wouldn't it?

To forgive is to have . . .

Feelings
Of
Revenge
Gone,
Inexplicably
Vanquished
Evermore!

You surrender your right for revenge, to treat others as they've treated you.

Matthew 18:15 says, "If your brother sins against you, go and show him his fault, just between the two of you. If he listens to you, you have won your brother over."

Could this be a misprint? Go to the person who hurt you? Who gossiped about you? Who tried to sabotage your work or your ministry, who bullied you or your family members? The one who tried to make you feel less than, unloved, and unworthy? Go to him or her?

As long as your physical or emotional well-being is not at risk, then, yes, that's what God says.

His Word continues:

But if he will not listen, take one or two others along so that every matter may be established by the testimony of two or three witnesses. If he refuses to listen to them,

tell it to the church; and if he refuses to listen even to the
church, treat him as you would a pagan or a tax collector.
MATTHEW 18:16-17

Some misread that Scripture, though. They translate this section as

If a brother sins against you, tell the church first. Then,
treat him or her as you would treat an outcast. If he or she
doesn't respond, then go to lunch and tell it to others so
that in the company of two or three witnesses, you shall
have closure and tasty desserts. Then, if you happen to
run into the one who has sinned against you, point out
his or her fault on the social media site or billboard of
your choice, and you will have won.

That's almost the same thing, right?

Sadly, many Scriptures are twisted to suit what's really in the
heart, aren't they? The fact is, some folks don't really want true
healing, repentance, grace, and redemption. They just want to win.

This reality reminds us of the notable performances by highly
trained and skilled actors acknowledged each year in Hollywood's
and New York's popular awards programs: Television performers receive Emmy awards, Oscar nods his approval for the year's
best performances on the big screen, and the Tonys highlight
Broadway's best. Millions of people around the world tune in to
the presentations to see the cream of the crop (when it comes to
acting or performing) receive their due.

If you're thinking heaven will be something like that, you
might want to return your designer gown right now. Tell the
jeweler you won't need to borrow the Hope Diamond after all.
Heaven's award ceremony is not going to go that way.

Our earthly award ceremonies and what will happen in heaven differ in a big way: God won't reward us for the roles we've played, but for what was truly in our hearts.

We all know people who talk as a friend to someone's face, only to bad-mouth that "friend" later on. It quickly becomes obvious that these people are holding on to grievances, judgments, and offenses, and they'll tell anyone about them *except* the person involved. Others act as if they care about someone's problem, when in reality they just want the "inside scoop."

Encouragement, authentic concern, and true love are always welcome. Simply excavating for details while feigning concern is transparent and hurts more than the questioner realizes.

Yet these folks seem confused by Jesus' words in John 13:35: "By this all men will know that you are my disciples, if you love one another." They interpret "if you love one another" to mean how well they *fake* love for one another in polite company. In other words, the world will know us by how nice we act in each other's presence, regardless of how we feel or talk behind each other's backs. This misses the point entirely!

Love, real love, weeps when someone stumbles. It bleeds when someone bleeds and feels for someone when troubles come. Unlike the fake love of some humans we know, God's unconditional love will always, always rejoice when people get back on their feet. Isn't our job to cheer each other on, especially the ones who fall?

To do that, our love has to be real. And that doesn't come by acting or pretending to get along. It comes by having the authenticity, courage, and freedom to talk with one another—to openly discuss our differences and seek true healing.

Whenever possible, God wants us to talk through a problem

or offense, clear it up, say what's true, and hug it out. We need to let it go and move on.

But forgiveness isn't denial. Too often, we jump straight to the hug and the moving on when we're not actually *able* to move on. We believe the wound will heal with all the dirt and shrapnel still festering inside, and then we wonder why the same wound keeps hurting year after year.

Granted, there are some situations where talking it through isn't possible. Reconciliation isn't always an option because it requires two people. But it takes only one person to forgive. God commands us to forgive, and He knows that doing so will bring a sense of peace. Just remember that you are *not* commanded by God to continually trust someone who has hurt you repeatedly. He or she will need to earn your trust.

If you need a reminder to forgive just as I did when I saw that billboard along the roadside, I can give you directions. Maybe that sign is still there, waiting for you.

If They Can Change You

If naysayers can dissuade you from following your dreams, they will make you as miserable as they are.

If the envious can convince you to hide your gifts lest others accuse you of showing off, those gifts will atrophy, and it will be as if you never had them at all.

If people can make you question your strengths, they will weaken you in spite of your power.

If your own doubts can convince you not to try, you'll never know how wrong they were.

If fear can stop you, the achievements that only you could have accomplished will be left uncompleted.

If day-to-day frustrations can shake your faith, then you will have nothing to stand on in the midst of a true difficulty.

If complacency can keep you focused on your own immediate comfort (or lack thereof), you will never experience the thrill of victory that comes through perseverance and growing pains.

If heartache, pain, difficult times, and disappointment can make you abandon your hope in God, then the enemy will have stolen your most valuable weapon against adversity.

CHAPTER 19

DOWN FOR THE COUNT

Every champion was once a contender that refused to give up.

ROCKY BALBOA

DO YOU EVER FEEL you're in the boxing ring of life, getting pummeled by a left hook, a right jab, and then a right cross, until you're lying face down on the canvas without any energy to lift your head? As you try to stand, you wonder:

What happened?

When you study your opponent, you realize how unfair the match is. You are outsized, undermanaged, outmaneuvered, and woefully underprepared.

Your internal dialogue isn't helping you either.

Watch out! He's coming back with more.

Duck! He's going to blindside you with a left hook!

She's going to pummel you, destroying whatever self-esteem you have left.

Run for the ropes!

Lie down and play dead!

"Why did you ever climb into the ring with this guy in the first place?"

You know instinctively that you must stand up and hold your ground. You're scared to death, but you do it. You determine that you won't back down from this confrontation. But you're spent! To be victorious, you will need backup.

You look for your tag team partner, but he or she is nowhere in sight. You're in the ring while your pal is buying ice cream at the snack bar after throwing you spiritual platitudes:

"God will never fail you. As for me, I'm outta here!"

"God said He'll never leave you nor forsake you. That was Him, this is me. See ya."

"Cast your burdens on Him. I've got my own problems!"

The bell rings, and somehow you manage to drag your sorry bones back into the ring where the pummeling starts all over again. You're out there without proper training, teeth protectors, and even the right shoes. (You might be wearing high heels!)

After each round, you struggle back to your corner where there's no water, no towel to wipe the sweat off your brow, and no one around to say, "Hey, you rest here. Let me have a go at it for a while!"

How did you end up in this predicament?

By mistaking an opponent, adversary, and deserter for your trainer, tag team partner, and friend.

Wow, you might think. *Really? It is that simple?*

Actually, yes. If those around you are there for the good times, taking what they can from you, only to flee to the hills when the hard times arrive, then you've chosen the wrong team. Or worse yet, you've taught the *right* team how to treat you the *wrong* way by your inaction, enabling, and apathy.

But wait a minute! Your image isn't even on that fight poster. What happened? You were up in the bleachers, reading a good book, enjoying your popcorn. You're a lover, not a fighter. You don't even like to watch the fights on TV. You watch tennis— table tennis. Even then, you have spasms of neck pain from the constant head turning—back and forth, left to right, right to left. You're in no shape to be facing down a prizefighter.

Yet, there you are in the ring with the heavyweight champion of the world! You know that because it is written on the back of his robe. And on the billboard. You don't want to be there, but there you are. You didn't choose this battle. It chose you, and it will have you in a choke hold until you whimper your surrender and give up whatever your opponent is demanding.

So how do you get out of the ring and back to your popcorn?

You call on the ultimate tag team partner—God. (Why would you trust such an important position to anyone else anyway?) Just turn and there He is, waiting with outstretched arms for you. He wants you to give the battle to Him.

Why didn't you see Him before? Was it because you were cowering in fear over the size of your opponent, so you didn't see who was waiting by the ropes to come to your rescue? Your Partner doesn't just have your water, your towel, and your back; He already has the championship belt. He's had this battle won since the beginning of time!

He will be with you just as He was with David when he slew the mighty giant Goliath.

He will be with you and provide a way of escape, just as He did for Moses and the Israelites when He parted the Red Sea.

He will turn what was meant to harm you into something for your good, just as He did with Joseph when his jealous brothers planned to kill him, and then changed their minds and threw him into a pit, and then changed their minds again and sold him into slavery. God's plan for Joseph happened.

God is waiting in your corner. Reach out and touch His hand. Tell Him you can't do it anymore on your own and you need His help. Step back and let Him fight the battle.

CHAPTER 20

LESSONS LEARNED
FROM BULLIES

I was bullied until I prevented a new student from being bullied.
By standing up for him, I learned to stand up for myself.
JACKIE CHAN

WE HAVE CERTAINLY LEARNED *more* from the encouragers in our
lives, but it would be wrong to say that bullies haven't taught us
anything.

In fact, to a certain extent we owe some of our success, whatever small measure we've seen, to the bullies in our lives: the
mean kids and their grown-up counterparts.

Their intent may not have been noble, but overcoming
the pain they have caused us has made us stronger. They've
inspired us to dig deep, to discover how much God loves us,
and to find our identity in Him—not in what others think
(or say) about us. They've inspired us to pour ourselves into
our work and callings, pushing ourselves to the next level
and the next one after that (after we stopped whimpering

and wallowing, of course). Being more, doing more, giving more, loving more, serving more—and forgiving more—than we ever imagined. And those bullies have given us the courage to stand up for and encourage others facing similar circumstances.

What Bullies Can Teach You:

1. *How to persevere.* Bullies don't give up easily. Neither should you (but in a positive way)!
2. *How to get back up when you fail.* Bullies are driven to see others fail. Be driven to succeed—and help others succeed too.
3. *That you are a person of worth.* You *must* be a person of value for a bully to spend so much of their time and energy trying to stop your good efforts.
4. *Where your strengths lie.* Whatever a bully is making fun of is likely one of your strengths.
5. *Who your true friends are.* Bullies will show you which friends have your back!
6. *Who you really are.* No matter which label a bully tries to give you, it doesn't define you.
7. *How not to waste your time.* Bullies want to provoke an emotional reaction. Don't bite their bait and give them one. Choose your response (your words or your course of action) wisely.
8. *How to guard your peace.* They have none of their own; they want to steal yours. Don't let them.
9. *How to recognize them and others like them.* (Even the wolves in sheeps' clothing.)

10. *That even a bully can change.* A difficult person can become healthier. (But not because you give in to them or allow them to disrespect or harm you.)

What better way to beat the bullies than to become all you were meant to be, in part thanks to them?

CHAPTER 21

PILLOW TALK

People gossip. People are insecure, so they talk about other people so that they won't be talked about. They point out flaws in other people to make them feel good about themselves.

BLAKE LIVELY

WHEN YOU STAY IN BED, you leave a vacuum in the "News about You" department. And these types of vacuums tend to be filled with worst-case scenarios. After a few "speculations" begin making the rounds, they start sounding like the truth:

"Did you hear Connie has a cold?"

"I thought it was colitis."

"Well, I heard it was E. coli."

"Ebola. That's what I heard."

"It was e-something. Or was that how I heard about it— through e-mail?"

"Maybe we should try calling her."

"Yeah. I'll use my iPhone. It's the only way we'll know the real story."

"I heard she changed her phone number."

"I heard she moved."

"I heard she died."

"If that's true, she probably won't pick up the phone anyway."

"I heard . . . Oh, forget it. I never liked her anyway."

See what we mean?

People are going to talk; that's what people do. And some of them will mix up the facts. (If you don't think that happens, just watch a political campaign.)

Be who you were meant to be, and do what you were meant to do. Don't worry about what the gossips think. After all, they are not living your life. You are.

You can't alter your decisions, plans, hopes, and dreams to suit every negative person in your life. If you do, you won't travel very far down the path that God has for you.

We say if they're going to gossip anyway, why not give them something good to talk about? Add them to your annual Christmas letter list and send a four-pager of positive news in eighteen-point type!

True Friends . . .

Care	Believe
Trust	Warn
Cheer	Help
Listen	Hope
Understand	Love
Remind	Laugh
Counsel	Forgive
Encourage	Defend
Embolden	Stay
Inspire	Bless

CHAPTER 22

DON'T TAKE IT LYING DOWN

A wounded deer leaps highest.

EMILY DICKINSON

IF YOU'VE EVER WATCHED a safari on the Discovery or National Geographic channels, no doubt you've witnessed a rule of nature: The wounded are free game.

Any beast of prey knows that he has to either wound the animal before the dining can begin or find an animal that has been wounded by someone else. Until the animal is wounded, he will use his full strength to resist.

The Bible says that our enemy is a hungry foe who is ready and willing to make a five-course meal out of the injured and bleeding. First the wounding, then the devouring—that is his plan.

When our spirits are wounded, we're easy prey. It's the bleeding that draws the devourers. If we're too slow to get back up on our feet, we're done for.

Granted, a Good Samaritan may happen along and help us.

But too often only the disinterested pass by, like the Levite and the priest who ignored the injured man in the familiar Bible story (Luke 10:25-37).

With a hungry lion on the loose, there's a good chance we could be lunch if we're wounded and don't get up!

The person who injured us isn't the only hungry beast out there. Others are just as hungry for a taste of the wounded. So do all you need to do to get back on your feet. If you need help, ask for it. Pray for it. But stand up!

Your emotional feet may be wobbly at first. After all, that bed on the side of the road has probably become pretty comfortable. But remember, the wounded gazelle attracts the vultures and the lions. The wounded gazelle that stands and leaps as best she can across the fields is the one who escapes her prey. Sometimes the lion decides she just isn't worth the chase.

But there's safety in numbers.

As soon as you can, find your way back to the herd, or to a new herd if the hungry lion lives or works (or worships!) in your old one. Your herd can be as small as one or two trusted friends, family members, pastors, or counselors. But two are better than one, and a group is less likely to be attacked. Lone gazelles are taken out more easily.

How do you heal? How do you learn to trust again once you've been wounded, especially if members of your own herd hurt you? Consider these suggestions:

- Realize we are all vulnerable and fallible. We can be wounded, and we can wound.
- Don't forget that life is tough for everyone, for the other deer and even the lions! A little understanding of someone else's journey goes a long way. (And you deserve understanding

of your journey as well. One-sided relationships seldom are healthy.)

- Project confidence! Don't unintentionally invite aggression with your passivity or tolerate it.
- Forgive the lion for doing what lions do. (But don't lie there and offer him another limb to chew on!)
- Embrace your need for community.
- When looking for a new herd, consider how they have treated others in the past, especially their wounded.
- Cherish your tested and true friends. (But be wary of those with fur in their teeth, especially if it's yours.)
- Learn from your past, but don't dwell in it. Were there any warning signs you missed or areas where you were vulnerable? Is there a way to spot emotional predators sooner and escape faster?
- As much as it is up to you, allow time, space, and opportunity for your wounds to heal. Don't pick at them. But don't leave the bandage on long after the healing has taken place. Band-Aids aren't accessories.

No matter what, don't let an emotional wound destroy you. Do what you must to stand again. Trust God, and then leap! (It's kind of like Zumba, only easier. And you can choose your own music.)

Return to living your gazelle life. You'll be a little faster, a little smarter, and a little stronger. Most important, you'll know that you didn't allow the devourer to win.

Say Enough Is Enough

Say enough is enough by standing, not by your retreat.
Say enough is enough through your triumphs, not by your defeat.

Say enough is enough with faithful friends—it just takes one or two.
Say enough is enough by making new friends if that's what you need to do.
Say enough is enough by not changing; don't let them make you hate.
Say enough is enough by rising above instead of taking the bait.
No one can make you be less than you are. So remember when things get tough:
The ones who matter will have your back when enough is enough is enough!

CHAPTER 23

WHENEVER YOU'RE READY

DIFFICULT PEOPLE ARE hard to face, whether we encounter them in our homes, workplaces, schools, churches, communities, or even our bathroom mirrors. But God's grace is sufficient, even for the most challenging relationship issues and the greatest personal crises. He'll help us navigate every practical dilemma, as well as our swirling thoughts and emotions, and bring us hope, healing, and victory!

Letting in the Light

Take some time to reflect on the following questions. You might want to jot down your answers in a separate notebook or journal (or on the back of a receipt or on the lid of a pizza box—whatever's within easy reach).

1. Which relationships or relationship issues (certain situations, confrontations, etc.) do you find most difficult to face? Has it always been this way? Is your ability to face difficult people improving or becoming worse? Why do you think that might be?

2. Ask God to show you if there is any hurt, bitterness, or unforgiveness in your heart. Is there anyone you have not yet forgiven or anyone whose forgiveness you need to seek? Jot down specific names or incidents that come to mind.

3. One by one, consider each name or incident you listed. Confess any sin or wrongdoing on your part, make the decision to forgive the person and release them to the Lord, and then pray for them. Pray about the next steps He would have you take toward reconciliation, healing, or moving on with your life.

4. If you list a particular person you cannot bring yourself to forgive, ask God to work in your heart. Ask Him to help you overcome whatever is keeping you from obeying Him in this. Pray about seeing a counselor or talking things over with a trusted friend.

Scriptures for Meditation

Let the morning bring me word of your unfailing love, for I have put my trust in you. Show me the way I should go, for to you I lift up my soul. Rescue me from my enemies, O LORD, for I hide myself in you. Teach me to do your will, for you are my God; may your good Spirit lead me on level ground.

PSALM 143:8-10

Love must be sincere. Hate what is evil; cling to what is good. Be devoted to one another in brotherly love. Honor one another above yourselves. Never be lacking in zeal, but keep your spiritual fervor, serving the Lord. Be joyful in hope, patient in affliction, faithful in prayer. Share with God's people who are in need. Practice hospitality. Bless those who persecute you; bless and do not curse. Rejoice with those who rejoice; mourn with those who mourn. Live in harmony with one another. Do not be proud, but be willing to associate with people of low position. Do not be conceited. Do not repay anyone evil for evil. Be careful to do what is right in the eyes of everybody. If it is possible, as far as it depends on you, live at peace with everyone. Do not take revenge, my friends, but leave room for God's wrath. . . . Do not be overcome by evil, but overcome evil with good.

ROMANS 12:9-19, 21

God is love. Whoever lives in love lives in God, and God in him.

1 JOHN 4:16

Pushing Back the Covers

Time to think about moving!

Choose one of the recommended resources listed at the end of this book to find detailed help for a specific relationship issue. These how-to books can help you find your voice, experience forgiveness, set boundaries, heal from past hurts, and build healthy relationships.

Using a study Bible, Bible study tools software, or a free

online concordance (such as BibleGateway.com or BibleHub.com), explore the Scriptures. See what the Bible says about the types of people and relationship issues you're wrestling with.

For example, if you feel worn down by too much trauma and drama, search for what the Bible teaches about rest and restoration. Or make a list of adjectives (with supporting Scriptures) that describe how God sees you. Here's a start:

Loved: Isaiah 54:10
Redeemed: Psalm 107:2
Worthy: Romans 5:8
Able: Philippians 4:13
Enough: Colossians 2:10
Unforgettable: Isaiah 49:15

Use the "Make Your Own Top Ten Lists" section at the end of part four to brainstorm snappy comebacks or positive, affirming, and life-giving responses to contradict the negative voices in your head.

Feet on the Floor

Try these first steps:

Write your wounded self a letter full of the supportive, encouraging messages you would say to a loved one in the same situation.

Spend time strategically thinking about your current relationships. Write in a journal, make a chart, and talk things over with a family member, friend, or counselor. Try to identify the biggest causes of hurt or frustration for you. Which behaviors, attitudes, and choices on your part or the part of others lead to that pain?

Ask yourself, *Do I see any unhealthy (or missing) boundaries in my relationships right now? What would healthy boundaries look like? What behaviors, attitudes, or choices would help me prevent crises or alleviate some of the drama and keep things from escalating in the future?*

Find a piece of picket fencing or an image of a fence and put it where you'll see it often. Use it as a reminder to make wise choices that will protect your heart, your mind, your time and energy, your family and friends, your ministry, or the meaningful work you do.

Likewise, if finding courage to speak up is your biggest challenge, buy a toy microphone or megaphone, or something that will serve as a visual reminder. (You could also record encouraging affirmations to yourself and play them back. Hear how you sound when you're brave!)

Choose a particular positive response to replace a negative response to personal pain this week. For instance:

When I (Christin) am tossing and turning and thinking of all the things I wish I'd said, I'll listen to Scripture or praise and worship music and have a quiet time instead.

I (Martha) will get up and start working, even if it's two or three in the morning. Working is productive; tossing, turning, and stressing isn't.

When I (Christin) feel overwhelmed by my failures and mistakes, I'll journal about how thankful I am for God's grace and how far He has brought me. Then I'll call, text, or treat for coffee someone else I can build up and encourage. When I find myself reliving the pain of a past experience that I've already processed many times before, I'll take a walk on the beach or read a good novel to change the channel in my head— instead of diving for the covers.

I (Martha) will browse bookstore shelves for a self-help book to find ways to improve the situation (at least in my own heart) or to see it in a different light. Or I'll chill at Baskin-Robbins (please see the heading titled "Life Lessons Learned from Ice Cream" in chapter 5). If I've experienced an embarrassing moment, I'll usually write about the humor in the situation.

And we'll both look for what God has taught us through it all. Don't think you know better than God! That difficult person may be in your life for a reason. You may be in his or her life for a reason. Never pay back evil with more evil. That's an addition problem that always multiplies your troubles.

God is just. He sees your heart and the hearts of those around you. He knows the time, place, and details of when you were hurt, overlooked, plotted against, misunderstood, or perhaps even failed. He knows the hearts of those who have let you down too. No matter how painful, there's usually something we can learn, something we can gain!

PART THREE

Facing Loss When It's Not on the Agenda

The greatest act of faith some days is to simply get up and face another day.
AMY GATLIFF

THE LONGER WE LIVE, it seems the more we have to lose. We face losing our health, our energy, and our physical beauty (or at least our youth). We can also lose our identity and our sense of purpose. We may wonder if hopes and dreams we once held dear will ever be fulfilled.

We may have lost jobs, homes, or a sense of worth or safety. Some of us feel we've lost (or are losing) all that was good in our country or our culture. We find ourselves saying good-bye to friends and family who are precious to us. Some are moving on and transitioning into different seasons in their own lives while others are stepping into eternity.

All this loss can leave us reeling. Maybe you've also felt

unable to face the thought of losing one more thing. Staying in bed just saves time on the return trips, right?

No. It adds one more loss: time. In this section, we want to remind you that somehow, in some way, you will survive your loss and find joy on the other side.

In your own time, by God's strength, you'll let go of your iron grip on those bedcovers and live your life again!

CHAPTER 24

WORKING IT OUT

I do twenty jumping jacks a day. Okay, half of that. I just clap.

MARTHA BOLTON

JUST THE OTHER DAY, I (Christin) was sorting through some old boxes that had been jammed in the back of the closet for years. In one box I found the little booklet that came with my very first crash diet: Richard Simmons' Deal-A-Meal.

So many memories came rushing back.

I remembered shedding a few tears as I watched the inspiring videos of formerly overweight women weeping in Richard's arms, thanking him for saving their lives. Later I shed a few tears when I tripped over the furniture and twisted my ankle while "Sweatin' to the Oldies." And the tears continued when I realized I'd used up all my meal cards for the entire day on a couple of slices of dried toast with a teaspoon of jelly. (I was so hungry, I started nibbling on the meal cards.)

I'm pretty sure I cried when I answered this question in the starter booklet: "Why do you want to lose weight?"

All these years later, looking at my answer, I felt such sympathy for myself I almost cried again. Very melodramatically I had declared, "I've never been so heavy in my life! I can't stand to live like this another day."

Then I looked at my starting weight—the number that had filled me with such shame—and fell on the floor laughing.

Oh honey, I wished I could say to my former self, *you have no idea. One day that will be your* goal *weight!*

Why is it I keep gaining the only thing in life I really want to lose? Name a "healthy eating plan" (aka "diet") or a frenzied fitness routine, and I'll tell you when I tried it. Lately I've added a whole host of antiaging strategies to the mix.

But no matter how healthy I eat or how much I exercise, no matter which ridiculously expensive beauty products I use, wrinkles keep appearing and body parts keep sagging. I'm forced to face the reality that I'll never look like those supermodels and celebrities I see in the magazines or on social media.

To be fair, some of them admit that they don't look like that either. Not without a whole lot of help from an airbrush. Alas, the magic of photo retouching doesn't apply to life in 3-D.

It can feel hopeless. So I ask myself, *Why bother? Why keep trying? Why not just give in to the inevitable? Why not just stay in bed in my pajamas and get really comfortable?*

It has to be easier than facing the reality that I'm not getting any younger, that I'm not as strong, healthy, or resilient as I used to be. It has to be easier than facing a past I can't undo and the fact that certain dreams were never meant to be.

I wish I could say it's a spiritual thought that keeps me from living in my pj's (one of those is coming in a minute). But it's not. I realize that if I stop fighting, if I climb into bed and surround myself with comfort food, I'll also give up on being the strongest, healthiest, happiest version of me that I can be. When that happens, I'll quickly resemble a different kind of woman, the kind on one of those TV reality shows.

No, I've decided if anyone will be cutting through my bedroom wall, it had better be a contractor adding an extra walk-in closet for all my fancy boots, not a team of paramedics and firefighters.

Actually, I'm learning that my battles in this arena have taught me valuable lessons.

While losing weight has been a struggle, I *have* managed to lose some spiritually unhealthy accessories: a few pounds of pride, self-righteousness, stubbornness, vanity, and immaturity.

My scars and wrinkles may not be pretty, but they've come with a little wisdom and a healthy amount of humility. And as my body moves south (to the floor, not Florida), it's doing so with much more compassion, understanding, and patience. I'm not strutting down a fashion runway, but I'm better at modeling God's mercy and grace. When you know how much you need grace yourself, it's easier to give.

See, I did eventually get spiritual. Speaking of which, here's a fabulous passage from the Psalms for all of us who feel tempted to pull the covers over our heads. It's an affirmation, a declaration, a proclamation, and a prayer all rolled into one:

As for me, I will always have hope;
    I will praise you more and more.
My mouth will tell of your righteousness,
    of your salvation all day long,
        though I know not its measure.

I will come and proclaim your mighty acts, O Sovereign LORD;
   I will proclaim your righteousness, yours alone.
Since my youth, O God, you have taught me,
   and to this day I declare your marvelous deeds.
Even when I am old and gray,
   do not forsake me, O God,
till I declare your power to the next generation,
   your might to all who are to come.

PSALM 71:14-18

It's also motivation to get into fighting shape (a much better motivation than a number on a scale, a preconceived idea of beauty, or a desire to fit a cultural standard)!

What does *fighting shape* look like? Here's my formula:

- making choices that are healthy for us spiritually, mentally, emotionally, and physically;
- getting enough rest and, yes, eating right and exercising (our bodies and our minds);
- drinking lots of water—the H_2O kind and the Living Water Jesus promised us; and
- spending time in the presence of God, in His Word, and with His people.

One of my doctors used to say, "God determines the length of our days; we determine the quality." In other words, in one sense, nothing we do will really prolong our lives. Our times are in God's hands, and He's given each of us a certain number of days.

What we *do* have some control over is how we spend those days and how miserable or happy, unhealthy or healthy they are.

I live with chronic pain, and some of it can't be cured,

treated, or avoided. But a portion of it can be alleviated, or even eliminated, if I do my best to follow my doctor's instructions and make healthy choices. These days I try to concentrate on what I can control to become the happiest, healthiest version of me I can be—for my own sake and for the sake of those I love.

Let me encourage you to do this too! It's important because you and I have a job to do. We need to pass on our faith to the next generation along with our hard-earned wisdom. Why let it go to waste? We want to be as strong and healthy as we can, for as long as we can, to accomplish all that we can for His Kingdom and His glory.

> I don't know about you, but I'm running hard for the finish line. I'm giving it everything I've got. No sloppy living for me! I'm staying alert and in top condition.
> I CORINTHIANS 9:26-27, MSG

And hey, will it hurt anyone if we look good while we're at it?

Top Ten Songs to Lift Your Spirits When You're Staying in Bed

Music has helped both of us gather enough comfort, inspiration, and courage to kick back that comforter and face life. Why don't you try it too?

The right song can remind you that you're not alone and enable you to focus on Jesus, count your blessings, or even slip off to sleep when rest is what you need most. Fun songs can even get you movin' and groovin' again.

Make your own playlist or bookmark some of your favorite music videos online. Here are a few of our suggestions (sacred and secular) to get you started:

Christin's Top Ten Song List:

From gentle to "gotta dance"!

10. "Be Still My Soul," David Archuleta
 9. "For This I Have Jesus," Graham Kendrick
 8. "There Will Be One Day," Cheri Keaggy
 7. "Up to Something Good," Honeytree
 6. "Oh Happy Day," The cast of *Sister Act 2*
 5. "This Good Day," Fernando Ortega
 4. "Pictures in the Sky," Rich Mullins
 3. "Up!" Shania Twain
 2. "Make Your Own Kind of Music," Mama Cass Elliot
 1. "Beautiful Day," U2

BONUS: When I'm bedbound, I often listen to soothing lullabies, including Michael Card's *Sleep Sound in Jesus* album, Twila Paris's *Bedtime Prayers*, and Kenny Loggins's *Return to Pooh Corner*.

Kathy Troccoli's *Come Just as You Are* and *Comfort* albums offer beautiful praise and worship featuring songs on the theme of grief and recovery. And Cheri Keaggy's contemporary Christian album *So I Can Tell* includes music written following a devastating personal crisis. Great music encourages listeners to lean hard on God's grace and find hope and courage to start life anew.

Martha's Top Ten Song List:

10. "I Never Lost My Praise," Brooklyn Tabernacle Choir
 9. "Come to Jesus," Chris Tomlin
 8. "What a Friend We Have in Jesus," Glen Campbell
 7. "No Longer Slaves," Bethel Music
 6. "10,000 Reasons (Bless the Lord)," Matt Redman

5. "Whom Shall I Fear?" Chris Tomlin
4. "You Never Let Go," Matt Redman
3. "His Eye Is on the Sparrow," Ethel Waters
2. "This Is Amazing Grace," Phil Wickham
1. "Don't Worry, Be Happy," Bobby McFerrin

Use the "Make Your Own Top Ten Lists" section at the end of part four to make a list of your favorite "feel-good songs." If you're feeling depressed, the list will make it easy for you to find an uplifting song.

CHAPTER 25

WHY?

Hard times don't create heroes. It is during the hard times when the
"hero" within us is revealed.

BOB RILEY

WOULDN'T YOU LOVE to have a T-shirt that simply said, "Why?"
You could wear it during those situations when that question
overwhelms your mind.

Why (did that person want to hurt me)?
Why (isn't someone encouraging me)?
Why (are times so tough)?
Why (did I lose my job)?
Why (did my husband leave)?
Why (did my loved one die)?
Why? Why? Why?

And the biggest *why* of all?

Why (is God allowing any of this)?

That last question can be the hardest. Why would a loving God allow such pain into your life in the first place or allow the pain to go on for weeks, months, or years? Why wouldn't He stop it? Or better yet, why wouldn't He have prevented it?

Often the answer to the *why* is this: It's for our own spiritual growth. Looking back on a few of our tough journeys, we can see we've learned lessons that might not have happened in any other way. On this side of the crises, we know we have

- received more courage;
- enjoyed more closeness with those we love;
- put less blind trust in the wrong people;
- put more trust in God's protection, plan, and love;
- gained confidence that all things will work together for our good;
- gained knowledge that God is in control;
- experienced God's faithfulness;
- witnessed answers to prayer;
- rested in His love;
- felt His peace;
- known His care;
- survived;
- and yes, even thrived.

CHAPTER 26

COULD POLLYANNA BE RIGHT?

Most people are about as happy as they make up their minds to be.
ATTRIBUTED TO ABRAHAM LINCOLN

WE CRINGE EVERY TIME we hear Pollyanna's name used as an insult. We understand why people do it. Regardless of its origin, *Pollyanna* has become a derogatory term today. It typically describes a person who is naively optimistic, intentionally blind to unpleasant truths, or willfully, woefully out of touch with the harsh realities of life.

But if you've ever read the original novel by Eleanor H. Porter or seen the Disney movie featuring actress Hayley Mills, then you know better. Pollyanna is so much more than she appears.

Porter's Pollyanna is a little girl whose father has taught her from an early age to cultivate in her heart "an attitude of gratitude," patterned on 1 Thessalonians 5:16-18: "Be joyful always;

pray continually; give thanks in all circumstances, for this is God's will for you in Christ Jesus."

Together, father and daughter play "the glad game," in which they try to help each other find something to be glad about or grateful for in every situation, no matter how difficult or unpleasant it may seem at first. Pollyanna's father, who is a minister, also teaches his daughter an important lesson that he confesses he had to learn the hard way: to always look for the good in others rather than focus on their faults and flaws. It's something that helped him become a better pastor and person.

As the story unfolds, the young girl experiences more than her fair share of heartache. Both of her beloved parents die, and she's sent to live with a wealthy aunt she's never met before, a cold and distant woman who dominates the social structure of an unhappy and unfriendly town.

In this unwelcoming environment, surrounded by negative, complaining, miserable people, Pollyanna proves that her spirit cannot be stifled or subdued. She daily lives out the truth of Philippians 4:4-7:

Rejoice in the Lord always. I will say it again: Rejoice!
Let your gentleness be evident to all. The Lord is near.
Do not be anxious about anything, but in everything,
by prayer and petition, with thanksgiving, present your
requests to God. And the peace of God, which transcends
all understanding, will guard your hearts and your minds
in Christ Jesus.

There's a difference between *pretending* everything is fine when it's not, and knowing everything isn't fine but *choosing* to focus on the good while asking for God's help. A true Pollyanna trusts in God's sovereignty, faithfulness, and love.

Just as her father taught her, Pollyanna looks for the positive in everyone and everything—and she finds it! With certain people it takes a little longer to do this, but she manages to bring out the best in everyone—from her aunt's housekeeper to the local doctor, the mayor, the minister, and even the town miser!

She teaches these new friends how to play the glad game. Her enthusiasm is so contagious that it spreads from one person to another and another. Even her hard-hearted aunt can't help but soften in response to Pollyanna's steadfast determination to rejoice and be glad. Pollyanna lives the words of Romans 12:21: "Do not be overcome by evil, but overcome evil with good."

In the end, when Pollyanna faces a loss that—for once— threatens to overwhelm even her resolutely cheerful spirit, the townspeople rally around her. One by one, they share with her how she has made a difference in their lives. They repeat her very words back to her: words of love and friendship, encouragement, hope, and faith. Her words had come from a thankful heart, a joyful heart, a heart that saw the whole picture yet chose to focus on the beauty in the details. Her lifestyle reflected Revelation 19:7: "Let us rejoice and be glad and give him glory!"

Yes, it's a charming piece of fiction, but Pollyannas do exist. There are people who look for the good in others, who comfort, encourage, and inspire. There are people who cheerfully choose hope, faith, love, and joy despite their circumstances. We like hanging around Pollyannas. It's inspiring to see the world through their eyes.

We're pretty sure theologian Dietrich Bonhoeffer would have agreed with Pollyanna. He said, "In its essence optimism is not a way of looking at the present situation but a power of life, a power of hope when others resign, a power to hold our heads high when all seems to have come to naught, a power to tolerate setbacks, a power that never abandons the future to the opponent but lays claim to it."[1]

We're going to play the glad game as often as we can. We'll look for reasons to rejoice—even in the middle of the hard stuff—no matter how silly or forced it feels at first. And we'll look for people whose hearts we can gladden with a smile, a compliment, an extra big tip, a helping hand, a hug, or an encouraging e-mail or text.

Say what you will about that sunshine-and-flowers girl— either of us would be proud to be called a Pollyanna!

CHAPTER 27

HAPPILY EVER AFTER

[My father] would get these far-off looks in his eyes, and he would say,
"Life doesn't always turn out the way you plan." I just wish I'd realized
at the time, he was talking about my life.

LUCY, in *While You Were Sleeping*

I (CHRISTIN) SPENT my eighteenth birthday in tears because
I was so disappointed with my life. I thought it was in ruins.
I'd been out of high school for two years already, and none of
my hopes and dreams were materializing! Life was not going
as planned. And there was no sign of a course correction any
time soon.

All through my twenties, I quoted Proverbs 13:12 to God:
"Hope deferred makes the heart sick." I was not so subtly blaming God.

"This desperate ache and gut-wrenching pain is your fault!"
I told Him. "It's no wonder I feel this way. You've deferred my
hope, so I have a good excuse for wallowing in my misery and
self-pity. If You don't want me to suffer, if You care about me at
all, You'll do something soon!"

I could have been referring to many circumstances. We all have to grow up and face the harsh realities of life eventually, and while our stories may not be the same, we can be sure each one includes disillusionment and disappointment.

But in this particular instance I was referring to my childlessness, caused primarily by my singleness. I won't recount the thoughtless and often cruel but well-meaning (I think) platitudes people at church offered to me about my single, barren state. From my late teens through my twenties and thirties, these people tried to be encouraging but didn't consider how their words would affect someone longing to be married with children. Some asked nosy questions and made ridiculous suggestions; others never had a real conversation with me but thought they knew what "my problem" was.

I won't tell you about every trite, clichéd Christian book that exacerbated my pain. They blithely promised that if I would (pretend to) stop looking, wait patiently, fix everything wrong with me, and find a place of perfect peace, contentment, and spiritual maturity, then God would bring me the perfect man.

I won't dwell on the grief, heartache, and loneliness I wrestled with—not for two or three years as so many singles ministry leaders do before they marry, but for decades. I won't mention every time I felt rejected by God—cast aside and overlooked— and every time I wondered why I was denied the blessings He gave so freely to just about everybody else.

In addition to those struggles, others seemed to see me as less of an adult, less of a woman, because I didn't have a husband or children. One church uninvited me as its retreat speaker when they learned I was single. They decided that I couldn't possibly have anything to say to married women.

I wasn't planning to speak on marriage. I was planning to

speak on what we all have in common: disappointment, heartbreak, and hopes deferred.

Here's what God taught me through those deferred hopes:

The answer isn't in a magical or scriptural formula that will fix the problem or make the pain disappear. God hasn't promised anyone a husband (or a better husband) or a baby (or another baby). God doesn't guarantee a more supportive family, a friend, house, job, or ministry. He hasn't pledged to provide perfect physical health, wealth, weight loss, beauty, popularity, or anything we think will bring us happiness or fulfillment in this life.

And if we think everybody else has all of the above, sisters, we need to look again. *Most* people on this planet don't have a fraction of the blessings you and I take for granted every day.

And what about those women who seem to have it all? I can tell you, after twenty-five years of women's ministry and stepping off the platform to hold sobbing women in my arms, another person's life is almost never as perfect as it appears. And if someone else has what you want or what I want, it may not necessarily be his or her dream. There are plenty of unfulfilled dreams to go around!

What's the "it" you're convinced will make you happy? What's the one thing you just can't live without? Let it go. Give it to Jesus, and do it for real—not because someone told you that if you do He'll give it back to you or give you something bigger and better in its place.

He might not.

Jesus doesn't promise to give you what you want. He doesn't promise you bigger and better. He promises you Himself.

And you *will* find that He is enough—more than enough. He's worth every battle, every trial, every tear you've cried.

When you let go of your heartache or deferred dream, when

you move past that, you'll find that the greater depth of your relationship with Jesus—the closeness and intimacy with Him— is worth the pain. Struggling, and then letting go, can force you to depend on Him in ways you never have.

And while there will be moments of anguish, there will also be moments when He comforts you so gently, so sweetly, in ways that are uniquely personal and meaningful to you! Your sensitivity to Him will increase as you come to know His voice and respond to it much more quickly. You'll be more aware of where He's at work in your life and the lives of others. And you'll become absolutely certain of His love for you and His ability to protect you and to meet your every need.

Your faith will become rock solid.

Unshakable.

That's the real gift.

I'm in my forties now, and I won't lie to you. There are moments when my childlessness still knocks me off my feet with a tidal wave of grief. But I've learned to tread water, to reach out for the support of my loving friends and family, and to count all the wonderful blessings of the very rich, full life and ministry God has given me.

And when I can come up for air and breathe again, I know that I wouldn't trade knowing Jesus the way I do, which has come (in part) through heartache and suffering.

This I Know

Remember the child's song that says, "Jesus loves me—this I know—for the Bible tells me so"? It's true, and there are many other facts about God that can be substituted for "loves me" in that refrain. Check out these verses and tell yourself, *This I know.*

God loves me—*this I know*—for the Bible tells me so.

JOHN 3:16

God calms me—*this I know*—for the Bible tells me so.

PSALM 29:11

God cares for me. 1 PETER 5:7

God laughs with me. PSALM 126:2-3

God weeps with me. PSALM 56:8

God helps me. PSALM 46:1

God leads me. PSALM 23:2

God equips me. HEBREWS 13:20-21

God delivers me. PSALM 18:2

God sustains me. PSALM 54:4

God protects me. PSALM 91:14

God defends me. LUKE 12:11-12

God saves me. ISAIAH 12:2

God sings over me. ZEPHANIAH 3:17

God delights in me—*this I know*—for the Bible tells me so.

PSALM 149:4

You might ask, "If God loves me so much, then why all the trials?"
Listen to Charles Spurgeon's answer: "Trials teach us what we are;
they dig up the soil and let us see what we are made of."[2]

CHAPTER 28

COVERED BY THE COMFORTER

Lord, if this is how You treat Your friends, it is no wonder You have so few!
ST. TERESA OF AVILA

THAT'S A NUN FOR YOU, keeping it real. We're trying to keep it real, too, because we want you to know we understand. We've both seen our share of troubles and heartaches. It comes with the territory, with being alive. Another nun, Mother Teresa, said she knew that God wouldn't give her any more than she could handle. Then the sweet saint added, "I just wish He didn't trust me so much."

Again, we know the feeling. Maybe you do too. Like us, maybe you've had your share of pile-ons, of troubles coming one after another, of wondering how God thought you could handle that much!

God's Timing

From the age of eighteen to my midtwenties, my (Martha's) life was a whirlwind of emotional ups and downs. I married and became pregnant. Regretfully, that pregnancy ended after twelve weeks.

I was thrilled when I made it to the ninth month of my next pregnancy and the week before my due date. It was during that appointment that my OB-GYN doctor couldn't detect the baby's heartbeat. He told me that he would be out of the country and would return in a week or so, and that if anything had happened to the baby, it had happened already. One week would not make any difference.

His words and lackadaisical attitude left me more than confused. But then, maybe he was of the opinion that nothing was wrong. At least that's what I told myself.

My diabetic doctor had a completely different opinion. He saw the urgency and said if my OB-GYN couldn't deliver the baby, he would do it himself. If something had happened, it was risky to leave the baby inside of me. Once my OB-GYN doctor heard of my other doctor's concern, he changed his mind. He scheduled a time to induce my labor, but then he let me know that I was "going to be keeping him up all night now."

I remember crying as he slammed down the phone, wondering which one of us was losing a baby. His reaction was so bizarre and hurtful.

After seventeen hours of labor and the tormenting silence of that fetal monitor attached to my stomach—waiting, praying for a fetal heartbeat (there's no quiet like that quiet)—I delivered a ten-pound-two-ounce stillborn son.

I was heartbroken, confused, and hurt. This turn of events made no sense to me. I couldn't understand why God had added this chapter to my story. I wanted to edit it out. Or better yet, rewrite it.

It didn't help that I was kept on the maternity ward, where

I would see the newborn babies being wheeled past my room. An unaware photographer even stopped by my room to see if I wanted a photo of my baby. But happier chapters, as well as more challenges, were still to come.

After the stillbirth, we applied for adoption. We had always talked about adopting, even if we had biological children. The stillbirth simply moved up that decision into the "now."

After waiting for what seemed like forever, God opened the doors for us to adopt a newborn baby boy. Within the next two years, God even brought us another baby to adopt, and at the time of his birth, I was also pregnant! Those were happy times, to be sure.

And then more complications arrived.

My pregnancy, which had proceeded relatively well, was now in jeopardy because of a condition called toxemia. But just after my husband had left the hospital that day, my doctors decided they would need to operate if my baby was to be born healthy. This happened in the days before cell phones, and there was no way to reach him.

So I was left to face this C-section alone, except for my doctors and the rest of the medical staff. Family would soon be on their way, but this was now, and I had to trust God.

All went well during the delivery, but then came another complication. After his birth, doctors determined that our baby had congenital heart disease and would later require two heart surgeries. The optimum time for these needed repairs would be when he was two years old.

What possible reason could there be for these complications? No one asked me if I wanted to be spiritually stretched like this, if I wanted to grow in my resilience and my faith. (If they had, I might have said no!) But it was happening. I hadn't counted on these plot twists in my story. They hurt! They didn't make sense. Every writer knows that a plot twist has to make sense. But God was teaching me to trust Him and His perfect timing.

On my own, my timing isn't always that good. At Bob Hope's funeral, I arrived just as a sea of Catholic bishops, priests, and cardinals in full dress were entering the rear doors of the church. Somehow, I was swept into their group, and I wasn't sure what to do. Then I heard one of the other writers call out from a distance, "It's okay—she writes religious books!"

In another example of my flawed timing, a comedian friend had sent me a smoked turkey for the holidays. I didn't realize that *smoked* meant "precooked," so I did what I'd seen my mother do: I put the turkey in the oven the night before and let it cook all night. When I removed the aluminum foil the next day, I was aghast at the shriveled, burnt-to-a-crisp bird. If I could have stood it on its legs, it would have resembled a Cornish hen on stilts!

So, yes, my timing is flawed, but God's, as I was soon to learn, is absolutely perfect.

During the time we were waiting for our son's surgeries to take place, he would inevitably get a low-grade fever on the day we were to bring him to the hospital. It was nerve-racking because if he needed the surgeries, then I truly wanted to be on the other side of them. But God knew what He was doing. Not long after the hospital had sent my son home and postponed the surgery yet again, I was watching the news on TV. A reporter announced that a doctor in the pediatric ward of our hospital had been diagnosed with hepatitis. Any children who had been at that hospital were asked to return and be tested for the disease. Our son didn't need the testing because he'd been seen by the nurse and then sent home.

Finally, our son received the two surgeries—about a month apart. It was during the open-heart surgery that a member of the medical team came to the waiting room and told me there were complications. They were uncertain of the outcome.

Immediately, I found an empty room in that hospital, got down on my knees, and prayed.

This time, God's answer matched my prayer, and our son successfully came through both surgeries. Today he is the father of four, including a set of twins.

We don't learn that God is faithful until something goes wrong in our lives. And God doesn't waste any experience, even mine! The story of my loss, the adoptions, and our "miracle" baby propelled me into a writing career.

My first published article was about the adoption of our first son. I was shocked to find a check for five dollars in the envelope, along with the acceptance letter. I remember thinking at the time, *They pay you to write?*

Now fast-forward more than three decades, when I was approached by a producer to write the stage script for a musical based on Beverly Lewis's book *The Confession*. The story is an Amish romance centered on (you guessed it) adoption. No one on the creative team realized until opening night that each one of us—the director, the composer, myself, and even Beverly Lewis—are all adoptive parents. I don't believe that was any accident. God had prepared our hearts to work together on that musical. Even others involved with the musical had similar connections with adoption.

Think about what you're facing right now. Could it be that God is teaching you something He'll be able to use later—not for your glory, but for His?

Let me quote a portion of Jeremiah 29:11 from the Bible

version considered by Bible scholars to be the most accurate:
large print.

> "For I know the plans I have for you," declares
> the LORD, "plans to . . . give you hope and
> a future."

It's true in large print, in smaller fonts, in braille, and in every
language on earth. You can believe it.

True Calling

There was a time in my life when I (Christin) had a hard time
believing that the Lord had plans to give me a hope and a future.
The hope and future I had envisioned just wasn't happening.

You see, I grew up with a deep love of family. We were always
close, but we grew even closer because of the tough times we
experienced together. My sister died of SIDS (sudden infant
death syndrome) when I was ten. My family moved more than
twenty-five times during my childhood and teenage years, faced
constant financial pressures, and was even forced to move in with
friends and relatives when a business partner betrayed my parents
and they lost everything. Throughout the years, my family also
served in one form of ministry or another, and we frequently
witnessed or suffered the pain and heartache caused by "CBB"
(Christians Behaving Badly). Through it all, we just clung more
tightly together.

I have such a large, close-knit extended family that I fully
expected to marry as soon as I was old enough and then start
a family of my own, with five, maybe six kids.

It was a shock when Prince Charming didn't arrive, no matter how many hours I sat wishing at the well or dreaming by the tower window. No fairy godmother appeared to whisk me off to the castle. And I didn't have a backup plan!

If I'm honest, deep down I knew I was meant to do something with my passion for God, for speaking and teaching His Truth, but I envisioned this occurring primarily in the setting of home and family. Instead, I spent years in what seemed like meaningless, unfulfilling jobs, miserable and unhappy, trying desperately to believe that somehow God was using all of it to help me grow! At the same time, I began battling chronic pain and serious health issues (some of which I've shared with you) while still grieving deeply the death of my most cherished dreams.

But God used the physical and emotional pain. He taught me about surrender, love, faithfulness, mercy, and grace. He was teaching me to desire Him above all else.

When I was in my late teens and early twenties, He started giving me opportunities to share what He was speaking to my heart. I began teaching women's Sunday school classes, Bible studies, and small groups at my local church, and then I started speaking in other church services and at banquets and brunches. I wrote a few articles for some magazines. They were published.

Now I look back at more than twenty-five years in women's ministry and a career that's included writing books, magazine articles, and blog posts; speaking at conferences and retreats; and hosting an internationally syndicated radio show. It's not at *all* what I dreamed or imagined for my life. But God made use of the twists and turns in my life, creating something beautiful from them.

The latest twist?

Prince Charming finally did show up last year. (He cooks,

so I've decided not to complain about the lack of singing forest critters offering to help with the housework.)

It's been an adventure itself, learning to share my heart and my life with someone else at this age while juggling the commitments in his life with the demands of my busy career and ministry. And don't get me started on the challenges of midlife wedding planning!

It's impossible for Martha and I to share all of our stories. Frankly, some are too painful still, and some we're continuing to process to find their purpose in our lives. But this book isn't really about us. And more important, we're tired of being sad about the sad parts.

(If we change our minds and decide to throw ourselves the mother of all pity parties, we promise to invite you. Especially if you can sing harmony on "Nobody Knows the Trouble I've Seen.")

We both know many other people who have suffered and lost a great deal more than we have, who have faced circumstances much more difficult than ours.

Whatever we're facing, we can almost guarantee that someone in the world has either faced a similar or worse situation—much worse. We're not minimizing the pain; we're just reminding ourselves that we're not alone in this human experience. We, and you, are not singled out for cruel and unusual suffering (1 Peter 5:9).

We've heard an illustration about an imaginary scenario in which we could all pile our troubles in the middle of the room and then choose from that pile the troubles we'd prefer to face. If we could see what others are facing, 99 percent of the time we'd gladly take our own back again.

The two of us have heard plenty of heartbreaking stories

over the years while traveling with our work, meeting men and women from many different walks of life.

Maybe one of those stories was yours. We're certain we don't have to tell you that there are no simple explanations for pain. Sometimes there just doesn't seem to be a *why*.

But in quiet moments, after some of the kicking and screaming has died down, the simple truth of God's love and His good plan can still speak to your heart if you're willing to listen.

And it can be powerful. Profound. Life changing.

Someone once said that the human heart is like a bucket. When it gets bumped, whatever's inside comes splashing out. In other words, our response to life's challenges reveals our hearts.

We can't think of a better biblical example than the Old Testament story of Job. God allowed Satan to bring calamity and disaster upon this righteous man to test him and prove his heart. In one day, Job lost all of his herds and flocks, the source of his wealth. His camels, sheep, oxen, and donkeys were stolen by raiders or destroyed by fire. At the same time, Job's ten children were killed when the house collapsed on them.

As Job heard report after report of ruin and loss, the Bible says he fell to the ground in worship—not in bitterness or rage, not even in suicidal grief: "The LORD gave and the LORD has taken away; may the name of the LORD be praised." Job did not sin by charging God with wrongdoing. Instead, he acknowledged God's sovereignty and affirmed his faith in Him. Job passed the test. It's obvious that Job's bucket was full of faith, trust, peace, and a spirit of humble submission to the will of God.

It may sound impossible, but we both know real people like Job. These good friends of ours have undergone extraordinary testing, excruciating suffering, and have "come forth as gold"

(Job 23:10). We want to be them when we grow up. We can see they've been comforted by the Spirit of God, the true Comforter. He has covered and wrapped them in blankets of grace and peace!

Seeing God care for them reminds us that the same all-sufficient grace and perfect peace is available to us—and to you. It's available today, for whatever we must face. Listen to what Jesus tells us in John 14:18: "I will not leave you comfortless: I will come to you" (KJV).

CHAPTER 29

WHEN LIFE'S NO BED OF ROSES

I have lived pain, and my life can tell: I only deepen the wound of the world when I neglect to give thanks for early light dappled through leaves and the heavy perfume of wild roses in early July and the song of crickets on humid nights and the rivers that run and the stars that rise and the rain that falls and all the good things that a good God gives.

ANN VOSKAMP

I (CHRISTIN) REMEMBER A TIME when I was in so much pain—physically and emotionally—that I just didn't want to be alive. My work was frustrating and unfulfilling, friends had moved on or moved away, money was tight, and my body was wracked with chronic and debilitating pain. Nothing came easily or went right. I felt so lonely. Life seemed dark and hopeless.

I knew I couldn't kill myself, but I wished that God would take my life. In fact, I prayed that He would. It hurt too much to go on living.

A friend tried to help me see that things weren't as terrible as they appeared, that there would be brighter days ahead. I wasn't convinced.

Don't get me wrong: I wanted hope. I just couldn't find any, and I couldn't stand the thought of any more pain.

God, I just can't bear it, I prayed. *I'm at the end.*

One day, after another long, teary heart-to-heart, my friend made me promise that every night for a month, I would list at least one blessing in a journal, just one thing I was thankful for. After all, Scripture tells us to pray continually and give thanks in every circumstance (1 Thessalonians 5:17-18). It reminded me of this old chorus:

> *When upon life's billows you are tempest tossed,*
> *When you are discouraged, thinking all is lost,*
> *Count your many blessings, name them one by one,*
> *And it will surprise you what the Lord hath done.*[3]

It sounded trite at the time. (This happened before the gratitude apps and thankfulness challenges and dares we see on social media these days.)

And I'll tell you, it wasn't easy. The first few days I wrote, "I can breathe, I can see, I can hear." And to be honest, I wasn't all that thankful for breathing, hearing, or seeing. Eventually my list progressed to "I have a roof over my head, a bed to sleep on, and my car still works, at least for now." But that quickly grew old. And a promise is a promise.

So I started looking for something (anything) good that happened during the day, no matter how tiny or insignificant, just so I could write in my journal:

I found a parking space close to the mall when it was raining.
I got a card [or a phone call] from a friend who wanted to

reconnect, someone who was thinking of me and praying for me.

My favorite praise and worship song came on the radio first thing, right when I turned it on.

I wrote down the little things, and then bigger things, one and then another and another. My journal filled with words about little miracles, answers to prayer, and the encouragement God spoke to my heart.[4]

My life didn't suddenly become a bed of roses. I was just looking for the flowers instead of the thorns. Now that I had eyes to see them, it turned out there were "roses"—blessings— all around me.

Step-by-step, I found ways to persevere. I looked for where God might be at my job, prayed for those I interacted with on a daily basis, and tried to make a difference in their lives. That approach made work much more meaningful and fulfilling. As I stayed positive and open to the possibilities, keeping my eyes open for other blessings God might have in store for me, I eventually found a new job that was a good fit for me: teaching at a Christian school. With it came a new church family and new friends. Month after month I watched as, somehow, the bills were paid. And I found a compassionate doctor who took the time to listen and promised to keep working with me until we found the right treatment for my pain.

In time, my faith was strengthened and my hope was renewed. My depression lifted. The psalmist had a similar experience:

I waited patiently for the LORD; he turned to me and heard my cry. He lifted me out of the slimy pit, out of

the mud and mire; he set my feet on a rock and gave me
a firm place to stand. He put a new song in my mouth,
a hymn of praise to our God. Many will see and fear and
put their trust in the LORD.

PSALM 40:1-3

You can throw a pillow at me if you want to, but I have to ask,

> *Are you ever burdened with a load of care?*
> *Does the cross seem heavy you are called to bear?*
> *Count your blessings, name them one by one,*
> *And it will surprise you what the Lord hath done.*[5]

I can tell you from my experience: Life is so much better when
you choose to spend your time smelling the roses instead of crying over the thorns.

CHAPTER 30

LIFELOCK YOUR JOY

Joy is the serious business of Heaven.

C. S. LEWIS

It was closing time at the discount store where my (Martha's) sister Melva was working. Her coworker had already closed the cash register and locked the money bag in her car so it could be dropped off at the bank on her way home. All that was left to do was lock up the store and call it a night. That's when she saw him. *That's the ugliest man I've ever seen in my life*, she thought.

Then she realized he was wearing a nylon stocking over his head, which contorted his face. She tried to remain calm, even as he pointed the gun at her and demanded money. She opened the drawer and took out what little cash remained, just enough to open the store the following morning. Then she did something that only Melva would do. She tried to "people please" him, no doubt to keep him from shooting her. It was *how* she did it that was so typically Melva.

"I'm sorry I can't give you a better robbery," she said, handing him the money.

But that was Melva. While she was often fearful and too timid to stand up for herself, sometimes she was unbelievably courageous. She was a champion of truth no matter the cost, a giving person who served others without reservation or agenda, a woman who preferred to laugh in the midst of despair, and who, in the end, had few possessions yet possessed everything that counted.

My sister Melva taught me more in the last year of her life than I could have learned at any Ivy League university. And she was still teaching me even after the doctors told her that she was losing her ten-month battle with uterine cancer.

"Is there anything else you want to do?" I asked her. Carol, our mutual friend from childhood, and I had taken her to visit the home where we grew up; the elementary school, junior high, and high school we attended; and several other special locations.

Melva didn't hesitate. She grinned and told us that there was one final thing on her bucket list: She wanted to "TP" (toilet paper) her daughter Eunice's house!

And there it was—Melva's idea of the perfect end to a fun-filled life. Melva had suffered more than her share of hurts throughout her time on this earth. She had plenty of memories of being left out, disappointed, misjudged, mistreated, bullied, and underappreciated. But she had survived it all, ultimately developing healthier boundaries, and now she was going out her way—surrounded by those who loved her, with her faith and her sense of humor intact.

Amazed at her unshakable sense of fun, Carol, along with my husband and I, grabbed a roll of toilet paper and helped Melva into the car. We knew her daughter Eunice and her family weren't home, so we hightailed it over to the house and got busy.

It was in the middle of the afternoon when we did our deed (seniors TP during the daylight). A neighbor, noticing us, drove by and leaned out her car window, laughing.

"Don't you know you're too old to be TP-ing houses?" she asked.

Melva's son-in-law and grandson said they were more than a little surprised when they learned Melva was the mischievous culprit. Melva, weak from cancer treatments, would have been the last person on their list of suspects!

About a week later, Melva, with a smile on her face and her Bible in her hand, was gone.

Melva knew she couldn't control her physical circumstances, but what she could control was her attitude.

On the wall next to her hospice bed hung three plaques. The first one featured the Serenity Prayer: "God, grant me the serenity to accept the things I cannot change, courage to change the things I can, and wisdom to know the difference." The second plaque said the very same thing. So did the third.

Melva wanted her life to leave that message. And she wanted this message to sink deep into her own life as well. Some things—as unfair and hurtful, as challenging and fearful, as difficult and unwanted as they are—just can't be changed. Other things have to be changed no matter how much courage it takes. And only God can give us the wisdom to know which is which.

Melva longed for that courage and wisdom. She was also determined to face her challenges with laughter.

This beautiful woman—who had done so much for others in the midst of her own needs; who had preferred to live in the shadows instead of the limelight; who had dressed up as a clown, Santa Claus, and the Easter Bunny entertaining countless children and the elderly alike; who had for years grown her hair for cancer victims and volunteered with the Red Cross to help with disasters—ended up looking death in the face and saying, "You are not stealing my joy!"

And it didn't steal her joy.

It couldn't.

Top Ten Reasons Not to Hide Yourself (or Anything Else) under the Bed

It's one thing to hide under the covers from time to time, but it's another to go crawling under the bed. As your friends, we have to warn you:

Don't do it!

Don't even think about it! There are distinct disadvantages to hiding yourself (or anything else) under there. Here are just a few:

10. Spiders
9. Big spiders
8. Hanging strings from the box springs look and feel a lot like spider webs.
7. There are dust balls under there—the size of big, hairy spiders.
6. Food is limited. And spiders have probably already chewed any food you do find.
5. You can start to feel claustrophobic under there, with those spiders all around.
4. It may be hard for the rest of the family to understand what you're saying in between your screams of "Spider!"
3. It's hard to move around, and besides, moving disturbs the spiders.
2. In the darkness, it's hard to see how much company you have (and by company, we mean spiders).
1. Did we mention spiders?

CHAPTER 31

CONSIDER THIS YOUR PERMISSION SLIP

Grief is like a long valley, a winding valley where any bend may reveal a totally new landscape.

C. S. LEWIS

GRIEF IS A JOURNEY we walk through in steps and stages. It's been said there are five steps: denial, anger, bargaining, depression, and acceptance. But that's a general observation of grieving people, not a scientific fact.

Not everyone experiences all five stages, and even those who do experience all five don't usually experience them in order, or one at a time, once and for all.

We've become so accustomed to discussing the grieving process in these terms that it's almost become cliché. Previous generations and cultures haven't always seen it quite this way. They didn't assign the same steps or stages to grief or expect anyone to move through it the way we expect to today.

And sometimes we forget: *Different people grieve differently.* Our journey is unique and individual to us.

Because there is no one-size-fits-all in the grief department, it may even be hard for *us* to recognize we're grieving. Our expression of grief won't look like anyone else's. We may bury it deep inside or mask it with self-destructive or superproductive behaviors. We may think we've simply been more irritable lately . . . or tired . . . or hungry.

Really, *really* hungry.

When we do see our grief for what it is, we have to face everything that comes with it: the full gamut of human emotions, tough choices, and harsh realities.

Just thinking about grief is enough to make us want to climb back into bed. But at some point (especially if we're staying hydrated), we will have to leave even the most comfortable mattress and answer the call of nature.

So we get up and start working through the recovery process.

Often our progress is not linear; it's not one step after the other. We tend to swing back and forth in our emotions, and we can spend more time in one stage while hardly any in another.

The process is as messy as an unmade bed.

If you tend to be a DIYer or a Martha Stewart wannabe, you may place a high priority on your bed being just so. You've coordinated the sheets and the dust ruffle to match the color scheme and arranged the hand-sewn throw pillows perfectly against the pillow shams. You always, always make your bed.

Or maybe you're at peace with a messy bed, but your husband is annoyed to see it with the comforter off to the side and the sheets wrinkled and mismatched. (How can he not see that the cracker crumbs spell out "I love you"?)

Whether it's you or others who are bothered by your messy bed (or your messy grief), we have a word for you: Messy is okay. In fact, we're giving you an official permission slip to be messy, and you can show it to anyone.* Not that you need anyone's permission, but we thought an official statement might be beneficial.

Your grief doesn't have to follow a pattern or the five stages. You can grieve in any way that's right for you. Forget what others think you should do or how you should act.

Grieve in the way that feels natural and healthy, for as long as you want, in whatever order you want.

You can stay in bed or find physically demanding work that helps you process your emotions.

You can journal or not journal.

Do you want to process the grief verbally, talking about it often, openly, and freely? Or would you rather process it internally, reflecting on it privately?

You can memorialize the grief with a special ceremony, activity, or trip. You can mark it with artwork you create or meaningful symbols you display in your home or office. On the other hand, you might not want to memorialize anything. That might not feel right for you.

You can focus on something positive. You might celebrate a life lived (as you grieve a death) or things you don't have to worry about anymore (such as bad hair days when you no longer have hair!).

Don't shame yourself—or let anyone shame you—for "not moving on" fast enough or for the opposite: not looking sad enough!

You can be messy. Your process can be messy. Life *is* messy.

Don't allow guilt trips, pressure, or a timetable for your grieving process.

---

* Terms and Conditions: (You knew there had to be some! We wouldn't be responsible if we didn't add this disclaimer.) If people you love and trust are expressing serious concern for your well-being, listen to them. Consider their input. Make sure you're getting wise counsel from somewhere and that you're taking good care of yourself throughout your grieving process. If you're doing that, then this slip is valid and can be applied to situations as needed.

Feel free to photocopy this page and place it in your journal or on a bedside lamp or bathroom mirror. Whenever you see it, take a deep breath and remember: You can leave your bed unmade today. You have a permission slip!

Permission Slip

I, _____, have permission to work through _____ in my own time, in my own way, without comparing my journey with anyone else's (positively or negatively), without feeling any obligation whatsoever to apologize for, rationalize, defend, or explain my process to anyone else. It doesn't have to "make sense" to anyone, including me. I will fully embrace the process, do the work it takes, and look forward to receiving healing as I follow the Shepherd of my heart wherever He leads.

CHAPTER 32

THE LIFE STRESSORS LOTTERY

If life were stable, I'd never need God's help.

FRANCIS CHAN

ACCORDING TO THE EXPERTS, there are about ten major life stressors that can easily send anyone into an absolute tailspin.

If you experience more than three of these in a twelve-month period, you've won the Major Life Stressors lottery! And you shouldn't be surprised if this major collision sends you to a counselor. (Seriously. You probably need to see a counselor if you haven't already.)

The insomnia, weight gain (or loss), crying jags, forgetfulness, distractedness, brain fog, depression, numbness, caffeine dependence, excessive sleep, or online shopping are not side effects of a drug advertised on TV. These are symptoms, er, *prizes*, from the lottery!

Want to double-check your ticket? Here are the winning numbers (in no particular order):

- Losing a parent, spouse, child, or someone close to you (loss due to death or divorce, an empty nest, moving away, or a falling out)
- Losing your job or career—or experiencing significant changes in your job or career
- Moving to a different home, city, school, workplace, or church
- Dealing with major health issues—yours or a loved one's
- Getting married and/or having a baby
- Facing financial stress
- Juggling substantial work and family-life commitments
- Experiencing stress in your environment (due to clutter, for instance, or conflict among coworkers or family members, or personal trauma, or anxiety due to world events, etc.)
- Feeling deeply unhappy about your personal appearance due to changes in your health, weight, physical abilities, or awareness of aging
- Feeling deeply dissatisfied with your life overall

Remember, just one of these qualifies you as a major life stressors "winner." Three or more of these stressors in a twelve-month period earns you the grand prize! Don't get too excited: The prize is only our empathy and an ironclad reason to stay in bed and pull the covers over your head.

While you're there, take a deep breath, cut yourself some slack, and call for help! You can start with a trusted friend or family member, someone who is a good sounding board and may be able to give you immediate, practical help with your day-to-day responsibilities.

It's also important to call an actual counselor, sooner rather than later. Do a little homework first. Online articles list questions you can ask to help determine what kind of counselor you need and whether or not a particular counselor is right for you.

Ask friends and family or your church for recommendations, or contact the Focus on the Family Counseling Department. You can speak to a Christian counselor there for free, Monday through Friday, 6 a.m. to 8 p.m. MT, at 1-800-A-FAMILY (1-800-232-6459).

CHAPTER 33

WHENEVER YOU'RE READY

IT'S NOT EASY TO FACE loss and grief and pain. Especially when one loss follows another and another, as so often they do. Truthfully, sometimes it's all you can do to collapse in the arms of Jesus and let Him carry you. You might even find yourself throwing a tantrum or two on your way to those arms and that surrender. That's okay.

But when you're done with the messy crying and you're ready for a glass of water and some tissues, consider trying out a few of the suggestions offered in this chapter.

Letting in the Light

Take some time to reflect on the following questions. You might want to jot down your answers in a separate notebook or journal (or on the side of a tissue box—whatever's within easy reach).

1. What significant losses have you suffered? Which ones do you think have affected you the most? Explain why.

2. From which losses have you experienced some healing, growth, or closure? Which losses are still raw?

3. How have you grieved loss in the past? Are you grieving now? (Even if you're not aware of it, would someone outside of the situation, knowing how *you* grieve, see evidence of it?)

4. Are you ever reluctant to grieve? Why?

5. What have you learned from your losses that may help others who are grieving?

Scriptures for Meditation

Yet this I call to mind and therefore I have hope:
Because of the LORD's great love we are not consumed,
for his compassions never fail. They are new every
morning; great is your faithfulness. I say to myself,
"The LORD is my portion; therefore I will wait
for him."

LAMENTATIONS 3:21-24

You, O LORD, keep my lamp burning; my God turns my
darkness into light.

PSALM 18:28

I will not die, but live, and will proclaim what the LORD
has done.

PSALM 118:17

Praise be to the God and Father of our Lord Jesus Christ,
the Father of compassion and the God of all comfort, who
comforts us in all our troubles, so that we can comfort
those in any trouble with the comfort we ourselves have
received from God.

2 CORINTHIANS 1:3-4

In this you greatly rejoice, though now for a little while
you may have had to suffer grief in all kinds of trials.
These have come so that your faith—of greater worth
than gold, which perishes even though refined by fire—
may be proved genuine and may result in praise, glory
and honor when Jesus Christ is revealed.

1 PETER 1:6-7

Pushing Back the Covers

Time to think about moving!

There's a time to grieve and a time to rejoice. Start a gratitude
journal or blessings poster on the wall or the fridge, use your
smartphone to snap pictures of special moments throughout
the day, or create a thankfulness tree for your home or office.
(For instructions, examples, and even more creative ideas, search
these terms on Pinterest or Google.)

Buy bedsheets decorated with roses (see the chapter "When
Life's No Bed of Roses") or choose another symbol of hope
(feather) or new life and rebirth (butterfly) to remind you that
life continues. Find a decorating theme that is meaningful to you.
Make a screen saver, collage, or necklace to keep that inspiring
imagery before you (Deuteronomy 6:6-8). You could even paint
inspirational messages on your walls or ceilings. Or use some of

those removable vinyl wall decals featuring Scripture or inspirational quotes, which you can find in any craft store or home goods department.

If your old dreams have died (or become unrealistic), find fresh hopes and goals for a new season of your life. Brainstorm a brand-new bucket list!

Feet on the Floor

Try these first steps:

Join a support group at your church or hospital, or a reputable recovery group online. Many churches and medical groups offer divorce care, grief care, cancer support, etc. Again, Focus on the Family also offers counseling. You can reach them at 1-800-A-FAMILY (1-800-232-6459).

Do something special in a loved one's memory. For example, make time to enjoy an activity, an experience, or a treat he loved; plant a tree in a memorial garden; walk a 5K to raise funds for a cause that affected her; or serve a community he cared about.

Remember, we all experience moments of discouragement, disappointment, hopelessness, and helplessness. These feelings often follow a crisis or trauma as well as major life changes and losses. Sometimes these moments can last for days, weeks, or even months.

If you've been displaying the following symptoms daily for some time, you might be suffering from depression:

- Feelings of sadness, emptiness, or unhappiness
- Angry outbursts, irritability, or frustration, even over small matters
- Loss of interest or pleasure in normal activities

- Sleep disturbances, including insomnia or sleeping too much
- Tiredness and lack of energy, so that even small tasks take extra effort
- Changes in appetite (often reduced appetite and weight loss, but increased cravings for food and weight gain in some people)
- Anxiety, agitation, or restlessness (for example: excessive worrying, pacing, hand-wringing, or inability to sit still)
- Slowed thinking, speaking, or body movements
- Feelings of worthlessness or guilt, fixating on past failures, or blaming yourself for things that are not your responsibility
- Trouble thinking, concentrating, making decisions, and remembering things
- Frequent thoughts of death, suicidal thoughts, or suicide attempts
- Unexplained physical problems, such as back pain or headaches

If you're showing these signs, see a counselor and a doctor. And as you begin to feel better, look for others who are not as far along in their journey and encourage them.

Consider turning your faith journey into a blog! Share your experiences with others who might benefit from what you've learned. But don't wallow—show how you are truly growing.

Gently, without bitterness, begin to show those willing in your church family and your community better ways to be supportive to people in crises. Lead by example.

PART FOUR

Facing Life—and Getting Yours Back!

*Lying in bed would be an altogether perfect and supreme experience if only
one had a coloured pencil long enough to draw on the ceiling.*

G. K. CHESTERTON

NOBODY SAID LIFE was going to be easy. The fact we started out
on this journey wailing our lungs out should have been a hint.
Many of us have faced circumstances that have shaken our faith
to its very foundation. On top of that, we still have to drag ourselves to work every morning or oversee family and household
matters while our challenges remain.

Is your to-do list as long as a selfie stick? Are you living in a
world where there aren't enough hours in the day, it doesn't seem
like you're making any progress, and the challenges you face
seem as high and as hard to climb as a mountain of king-sized
mattresses? You might be thinking, *Why not surrender to the stress
and just stay in bed?*

Why? Because—take it from us—procrastination, avoidance,

or numbness only makes things worse. Much, much worse. And waiting for someone else to encourage or help you may leave you waiting a long time.

In this section, we'll share what helps us when we feel overwhelmed. You'll find ideas, encouragement, and strategies to help you rediscover your get-up-and-go.

CHAPTER 34

DON'T PILE 'EM HIGH

I live before the Audience of One. Before others I have nothing to prove,
nothing to gain, nothing to lose.

OS GUINNESS

I (MARTHA) LOVE BUFFETS. I love piling my plate up with samples of just about everything offered on the serving tables and eating myself into a cholesterol coma. Well, not exactly a coma. It's more like a very deep nap—a *noma*.

I don't eat like that every day, only at buffets. There's something about buffets that invites you to overeat. The government has yet to require buffets to install a machine that can calculate the calorie count for each plate, but if that happens, the numbers will be spinning faster than the ones on the national debt clock!

Have you noticed that some of us tend to approach life this way? Whether we dish it up ourselves or someone else has added those extra items (with or without our consent), our plate is full. We're overworked, overcommitted (primarily because we can't say no), overwhelmed, and underappreciated. We start to feel burned out.

Then, as if we don't already have more than we can handle, life comes along and throws on another drumstick or a second slice of apple pie. What's the difference to the person who can eat—I mean, do it all?

If there's a towering, teetering pile of responsibilities on our plates, we might need to put our forks down and reassess things: Which items are truly worth our energy and efforts? Which could we do without? And which things could we leave for others who have more room on their plates?

Stop for a moment and consider this popular saying: "Just because you can doesn't mean you should." Are the good things on your list unnecessarily taking time away from your family? Are they taxing your own strength and energy? Is there an item or two that would help someone else grow their own skills as they do the task?

As you review each task, ask yourself a few more questions: *Will my work enable someone else's irresponsibility or cover for their lack of effort? Is my work truly needed or wanted? Is someone taking advantage of me? Are my talents better used elsewhere?*

Start resisting the urge to pile your plate too high, or you'll find yourself quitting, crashing, falling into a deep depression, or collapsing into bed.

If you can find your bed underneath all the cute throw pillows, that is. I (Christin) must be one of the few women who don't own a stack of those silly, frilly things.

And that's mostly because I can't stand the futility. I don't understand why you'd want to waste years of your life (collectively) piling them on your bed in the morning, only to pile them on the floor in the evening, only to pile them back on the

DON'T PILE 'EM HIGH

bed the next morning. Unless maybe it's for the exercise? They don't look like they weigh enough to help you develop much muscle tone.

But just as I start judging, I remember the pile of sticky notes on which I write my to-dos, a ridiculously long list of tasks I can't hope to accomplish in a month, let alone a day. I just move the sticky notes from one calendar page to the next, day after day.

Yet I wonder why I feel so exhausted and overwhelmed! Ironically, it takes me only three days to watch seven seasons of my new favorite Netflix show.

(My family says "creative avoidance" is my superpower. I say watching TV isn't that creative; creative is what I'm going to do to them as soon as I finish this next episode.)

Pass me a pillow, would you?

Seriously, what are we trying to prove, and whom are we trying to please or impress? Why do we impose these unrealistic expectations and impossible standards on ourselves?

We've read enough self-help and spiritual-life books to suspect it has something to do with our insecurities and self-worth, as well as our desire to be loved and accepted by others. In this misguided attempt, we become *human doings* rather than *human beings* in order to "earn" acceptance.

If we stop and take a closer look, we may discover that we've even been trying to gain God's love, to prove ourselves worthy of His grace and deserving of His time and attention. That's when it helps to revisit the Scriptures that remind us we can do absolutely *nothing* to earn God's unconditional love. We need to remember how much He cares for us—just as we are—and how committed He is to doing what's best for us. Sometimes it takes getting to the end of ourselves and all of our "doings" to learn to rest in the love He has for us (1 John 3:19-20).

CHAPTER 35

REFRAMING THE SITUATION

Life is ten percent what you make it, and ninety percent how you take it.
IRVING BERLIN

YEARS AGO, when our new home was being built in a different state, I (Martha) was buried in deadlines and couldn't check the construction site with my husband. He went alone, with instructions from me to take plenty of photos of the progress.

When he returned and we developed the photos, I was surprised to see how he'd carried out my instructions. Amazed, really. I was particularly taken aback by the photo angles.

Very few pictures included the house or showed the progress of the construction, the framing, or anything else.

The photos were mainly of vistas beyond the house. My husband had photographed the views from each window opening. He wanted to show me what we would see every morning as we looked out of our bedroom window, the living room window, the kitchen window, and so on. That's because he was focused on the future and the finished product, not on the work left to be done.

Too often, as we focus on our tasks and to-dos, the problems we have and the ones we anticipate, we lose sight of the finished product. We concentrate so hard on the work ahead of us—taping the drywall, staining the trim, grouting the tile—that we can no longer visualize the end goal!

I can't help but wonder what our lives would be like if we reframed how we thought about our tasks and to-do lists. Can we change our focus?

What if we concentrated less on the problems and potential pitfalls and more on the outcomes we're praying for and working toward?

What if we deliberately angled our lenses to emphasize the positive, no matter where we are in the process?

What if we regularly took time to stop and see how far we've come, and then gave thanks for our progress?

Until reality matches our desires and dreams . . . until our loved one is healed, a prodigal returns home, challenges are met with understanding and encouragement instead of judgment and apathy, and our own bodies are made whole, it is our choice to focus on either the problems or the resolutions, the answers or the questions, the successes or the failures.

Let's angle our cameras so we always see the view outside our windows. The house may not be finished as quickly as we'd like, but in the meantime, we can choose our daily view. Will it be the mess of the construction site or the scenery of tomorrow?

CHAPTER 36

ON THE ROAD AGAIN

Not merely does God will to guide us in the sense of showing us his way,
that we may tread it; he wills also to guide us in the more fundamental
sense of ensuring that, whatever happens, whatever mistakes we may make,
we shall come safely home.

J. I. PACKER

SOMETIMES TROUBLES MULTIPLY. You've probably already noticed that, haven't you?

My husband and I (Martha) were reminded of that truth one winter when we were trying to schedule a post-op appointment following surgery on my left eye. That was the start of the troubles, I suppose—my need for surgery in the first place.

Then a second problem happened along. On the day of the appointment, a historic ice-and-snow storm rolled into our area. From the moment we left our driveway, the roads were a mess, and salt trucks and snowplows were nowhere to be found.

A block from our house, our car slid on the ice, which probably should have been our hint to return home, but we pressed on, working our way into the grooves in the ice left behind by the other drivers determined enough to brave the roads that day.

As we merged onto the highway, our troubles intensified with huge flakes of snow continuing to cover an already blanketed landscape, making it practically impossible to see. Then came the next challenge in our already challenge-filled day.

The driver's side windshield wiper froze. It stopped right in its icy tracks. This wiper had worked fine during the last rainstorm, come through a rough-and-tumble car wash in good condition, and even efficiently removed the bug that had thrown itself against our windshield in a desperate attempt to go out with a splash. But now, in an epic snowstorm, it quit on us!

At least the wiper on the passenger side was still working. As the snow piled up, obliterating my husband's view, I navigated with my one good eye, leaning forward to peer through my side of the windshield, telling him to steer a few inches to the right, a few to the left, and so on down the road, desperately searching for the exit sign so we could take the off-ramp.

But then the windshield wiper on my side froze. Now with no working wipers, neither one of us could see.

We couldn't roll down the windows because the electrical wiring for the controls had malfunctioned, and we hadn't gotten around to fixing it. Changing lanes to move to the shoulder was risky because it entailed getting out of the groove and driving onto the roadway where ice hidden under snow awaited unsuspecting drivers. Even though we couldn't see, we had no choice: We had to get off the highway. So we slowly, cautiously, and prayerfully made our way across several lanes to the nearest exit.

Then, just as we maneuvered down the ramp, we hit a patch of ice and lost control, sliding toward the cars in front of us. To avoid hitting them, my husband turned the wheels sharply, and we careened into the ditch.

By the time we managed to get the car out of the ditch, the

storm had worsened. It was time, we decided, to abort the mission. The journey home was also treacherous, but had we kept driving to our destination, we would have been returning home in much more dangerous conditions.

Thankfully, we finally made it home safely that day. But we did so only because we were willing to adapt and adjust our plans. And we prayed quite a bit too.

If we know God, trouble is a fine reminder to pray and remember "from whence cometh our help" (Psalm 121:1-2, KJV). And sometimes He advises us to turn around.

Asking for God's guidance and learning to trust Him reminds me of driving with GPS. You learn to trust the map and the guidance system, discovering that when you miss a turn or make a mistake, you can always "recalculate" or turn around if need be.

Maybe you've heard of "God's GPS":

Give thanks.
Pray continually.
Submit your plans to Him joyfully.

Ask Him to take the wheel. He always leads us faithfully; His guidance is trustworthy and dependable. And if we will learn to "recalculate"—be flexible, adaptable, and teachable—we'll discover great joy in the journey, despite the obstacles we face.

CHAPTER 37

MORE THAN YOU PRAYED FOR

More things are wrought by prayer than this world dreams of.
ALFRED LORD TENNYSON

GOD ANSWERS OUR PRAYERS. Major ones. Minor ones. Prayers
you pray every day, and some you mention in a moment of crisis
and then forget—until one day you realize that every challenge
that has come your way since was a direct result of that crisis
prayer. It may not have been the answer you wanted, but it was
the one you needed. And sometimes you may only be able to
call out one word—the name "Jesus!"

Maybe you prayed for courage to stand up in a certain situation. Or you prayed for wisdom, favor at work, or more time to
spend with your family. You fully expected God to part the Red
Sea of your fear, your heartache, your overloaded schedule, the
unfairness of life, and make everything right. That's not always
how it works. You may have found that out.

Instead of changing the situation you're in, sometimes God

will allow even more such situations to occur, situations that will help you grow the muscles you need to tackle those types of circumstances in the future.

We have both prayed for courage to deal with difficult people or stand up to bullies in our lives. What did we get? A few more bullies and difficult people to deal with. We prayed for wisdom. What did we get? More challenging experiences that caused us to develop wisdom. We prayed for favor in our work. What did we get? Tougher assignments that required us to learn new skills and stretch our talents and vision.

(For goodness' sake, whatever you do, do *not* pray for patience—or more compassion for those who are suffering—or, well, you get the idea!)

In the end, God did answer our prayers. We can look back and see that our courage has in fact increased. It's not where we'd like it to be, but we know the process now and can kick it into gear when we need it. We continually pray for wisdom. We all need that 24-7. Our faith has increased too.

And we actually look forward to new opportunities to grow. If you're smart, you never stop learning. You can learn from those with more experience than you have, as well as those with less. You can always, always learn. (One thing we've learned is to count all of our life experiences as "material"—we'll use most of it in a book somewhere!)

Whatever you're praying for, know that when you pray, God will answer your prayer. Maybe not in the way you're expecting, but in a way that will help you grow in the areas you need it most.

CHAPTER 38

THE PROVERBS 31 WOMAN
REVISITED

She can laugh at the days to come.

PROVERBS 31:25

Is IT JUST US, or does the Proverbs 31 woman seem like a bit of a
show-off? We mean, really—who among us can hope to measure
up to this scriptural paragon of perfection? She's like that cheerleader in high school who had the greatest hair, the straightest
teeth . . . and could not only do the splits but also stand up
afterward. (If we had tried the splits in tenth grade, we wouldn't
have stood up until the eleventh.)

Reading the accomplishments of this woman (the Bible character, not the cheerleader) can be discouraging. While the rest of
us are looking for courage to face the day, she's already up and
at 'em, setting new standards of achievement that make her the
original "Wonder Woman."

In thinking about it, though, there may have been a mis-
understanding. Some cultural information was lost in translation.

Of course, we agree that the Proverbs 31 woman is nearly perfect. But the way *we* read her chapter, those noble attributes are actually more attainable than we might think. We've imagined what they might sound like in a more contemporary Bible translation that has yet to hit the market.

We're not saying this is the *correct* translation. But it does make us feel better about ourselves.

For instance:

The heart of her husband doth safely trust in her. . . .
She will do him good and not evil all the days of her life
(KJV ff. ital).

Our translation: She shall not yank the blankets to her side of the bed with such force that he doth tumble to the ground.

She seeketh wool, and flax.

Not satin for sheets, lest both she and her husband slideth off in the middle of the night. Avoideth thou it!

She is like the merchants' ships; she bringeth her food from afar.

Chinese take-out is perfectly acceptable—preferable even.

She riseth also while it is yet night, and giveth meat to her household, and a portion to her maidens.

Midnight refrigerator raids are a noble thing!

She girdeth her loins with strength, and strengtheneth her arms.

To us, this one sounds like exercise. But we double-checked, and there is no mention of Pilates in Scripture, or push-ups for that matter. So what to make of that "strengtheneth her arms" verse?

Could this be one of the earliest warnings of the dangers of loose underarm skin? We figure it must have been a concern even back then. Riding around in those open-air chariots would have led to fierce flapping of underarm flesh. Painful *and* unsightly.

We don't see underarm flab in ancient statuary (Venus de Milo doesn't have any). So it would seem in this Scripture that we're exhorted to do a little exercise to "strengthen our arms." And also our loins, but we think that is a forewarning of the stamina we would need once Spanx body shapers, panty hose, and leggings came on the scene.

But we could be wrong.

Moving on . . .

She perceiveth that her merchandise is good.

She knoweth her own value and valueth her own worth. No low self-esteem here.

Her husband is known in the gates, when he sitteth among the elders of the land.

Behind every good man is a good woman. (And you didn't think *that* was in the Bible!)

She maketh fine linen, and selleth it; and delivereth girdles unto the merchant.

Now, this one is a little trickier to pull off (much like most girdles). Delivering a girdle to anyone is bound to go badly.

"I was just passing by and felt led to give this girdle to you. Have a blessed day."

"Here, you look like you could use this. Bless your heart."

"We're from the Visitation and Girdle Committee. We want to welcome you to our church. Would you like your girdle in ivory or midnight black?"

She looketh well to the ways of her household, and eateth not the bread of idleness.

We're not sure, but we think this verse may foreshadow gluten-free living; then again, going completely gluten-free is ridiculously hard work. (If we're wrong on that, we'll eat our words. They're gluten-free.)

Her children arise up, and call her blessed; her husband also.

The biggest challenge here is getting the husband and children to *arise*. As for being called blessed, just don't expect that to happen when you're trying to get them to "arise."

And he praiseth her.

Clear instruction that she's to *receive* thoughtful birthday, anniversary, holiday, thank-you, and friendship cards and gifts throughout the year.

Give her of the fruit of her hands.

She shall receive equal pay.

And let her own works praise her in the gates.

She hath the highest-rated handmade-crafts shop on Etsy!

See? No need to stress over how to be the perfect Proverbs 31 woman. It's all in how you read it. And not only that, it's important to remember that this chapter describes an *ideal* woman. This list was originally compiled by a good woman in Bible times to teach her son how to find a good woman of his own!

Then again, maybe being a Proverbs 31 woman *is* attainable in the highest sense, the truest sense, the most spiritual sense. Perhaps it's possible to have the *heart* of the Proverbs 31 woman.

Of all her ideal qualities, the one mentioned in verse 30 is by far the most important: "Charm is deceptive, and beauty is fleeting; but a woman who fears the LORD is to be praised."

So who is the woman to be praised? A woman who reverences and respects God, who gives Him first place. A woman who looks to Him, loves Him, and serves Him with all she is and all she has. A woman who makes a positive difference in the lives of those in her care.

That's the kind of woman we each aspire to be.

We're still learning every day what this looks like in our

own lives. But this we know: God doesn't want us stressed out, overworked, underpaid, exhausted, and underappreciated. He doesn't want us so overwhelmed at the thought of trying to do it all that we do nothing and we just take to our beds instead!

The Message offers this paraphrase of Jesus' words in Matthew 11:28-30:

> Are you tired? Worn out? . . . Come to me. Get away with me and you'll recover your life. I'll show you how to take a real rest. Walk with me and work with me—watch how I do it. Learn the unforced rhythms of grace. I won't lay anything heavy or ill-fitting on you. Keep company with me and you'll learn to live freely and lightly.

As the Proverbs 31 woman could tell you, that's an offer too good to refuse!

Top Ten Reasons to Come Out from Under the Covers

10. Under the covers, it's hard to tell the difference between the buzz of a mosquito and an incoming missile. You might find yourself overreacting or "underswatting."
9. No one takes you seriously when you spend your days in adult onesies.
8. The shopping is seriously limited.
7. As Shakespeare or somebody (we can't remember) once said, "Cookie crumbs make bad bed pillows." (Oh yeah, it was our husbands.)
6. Nature is never going to give up and stop calling.
5. No one can see how saintly you've become because of all of your suffering.

4. Out from under your benevolent but watchful eye, your friends and family have free rein to do whatever they want. (As the psalmist said, "Selah—think about that one for a minute.")

3. Bedposts aren't the kind of boundaries your counselor was talking about.

2. The air gets a little (how can we put this delicately) stale? You don't notice that unique "aroma" after a while, but other people do. Take it from us; you *really* need fresh air—and the fresh perspective that comes with it!

1. Lying there, day after day, counting the threads in your bedsheets is just plain boring. You have a life to live. It's time to get on with it!

CHAPTER 39

PULL THE PILLOW *AWAY* FROM YOUR FACE

Courage doesn't always roar. Sometimes courage is the quiet voice at the end of the day saying, "I will try again tomorrow."

MARY ANNE RADMACHER

I (MARTHA) LOVE RISING EARLY. It's usually still dark outside when I start my day, but it's quiet inside, and I can accomplish a great deal of work. It's in the darkness that I hear the morning birds. It doesn't matter if I'm feeling the pressure of a deadline, am frustrated that my computer is acting up, or troubled about something; the moment I hear the birds, life is better. Their songs pierce the darkness and any frustration or trouble I'm facing. They bring me comfort, because if they're singing, I know a new day isn't far behind.

Those birds don't listen to anyone who asks, "Why are you singing? Don't you realize daybreak might not ever come? There are no guarantees in life!"

You can't say that to a bird. He'll just stare at you and chirp anyway. He knows that he knows that he knows that morning comes every day. Even if it's stormy, morning still comes. Even if his nest isn't as fine as his neighbor's in the mighty oak tree next door, morning is still coming. Even if his feathers aren't as full or as colorful as the other birds' plumage, morning always returns, and it's time for his song! Birds don't let anything hold them back from singing. Even in the dark. They know daylight is just around the corner. It's time to sing!

I've learned a lot from these morning birds. They're fully awake, ready to greet the new day. Instead of grumbling about whatever's not working in their lives or the discomfort of the twigs in their nests, they're *singing*! Another bird may have stolen their worms the day before, but they're singing. Some of their eggs might not have hatched, but they're singing. They might even have injured wings, but they're singing.

I don't always sing in the middle of the darkness. I might worry or try to process my feelings. I pray. But sing? That's not an easy thing to do, especially after an unsettling dream, an encounter with a difficult person, a medical challenge, or an unexpected loss.

When I was fourteen, a phone call delivered news no one ever wants to hear. My best friend had died. I felt a deep sense of loss for years, and I still think about her to this day. I still wonder how different life might have been had she still been here, as close as a phone call or visit.

I wish I could travel back in time and tell my friend that whatever she was feeling, life would seem more manageable in the morning. The darkness cannot stay, not in the presence of the sun. Hopelessness may lurk in the night doing its best to discourage us, but when the morning comes, the light will send it on its way.

I've felt plenty of pain in my life, and I've had times when I just wanted that pain to end. After our baby's stillbirth, I came home to an empty nursery, but the baby magazines came in the mail for months. I'd run into well-intentioned friends who would excitedly ask if I'd had a boy or a girl, completely unaware of what had happened.

How do we sing through life's challenges? Christin and I have learned that we need to continually remind ourselves to think about "whatsoever things are lovely" as Philippians 4:8 (KJV) tells us. That chapter also commands us to "rejoice in the Lord always." Rejoicing and singing—they go together, don't they? Find something to rejoice in, even if it's that strong cup of coffee or hot tea in the morning.

The promise of tomorrow has kept me steady through the hard times. I've always held on to the belief that no matter how dark the night, sunrise always arrives on schedule. It always, always, always comes. This belief may sound simple, but it's important to keep it in our heads and hearts.

We can't despair.

Part of the problem may be our misguided expectations that life should be fair and pain-free, that there won't be disappointments, losses, rejections, bullies, or any other difficulties that we know all too well come with the package called life. Many of us eagerly read the Bible looking for the Scriptures about peace and love while we skim over the mention of the great challenges faced by many biblical figures.

The apostle Paul tells us,

> We do not lose heart. Though outwardly we are wasting away, yet inwardly we are being renewed day by day. For our light and momentary troubles are achieving for us an eternal glory that far outweighs them all.

2 CORINTHIANS 4:16-17

A few chapters later, he mentions some of his own "light and momentary troubles":

> Rather, as servants of God we commend ourselves in
> every way: in great endurance; in troubles, hardships
> and distresses; in beatings, imprisonments and riots;
> in hard work, sleepless nights and hunger . . . through
> glory and dishonor, bad report and good report; genuine,
> yet regarded as impostors; known, yet regarded as
> unknown; dying, and yet we live on; beaten, and yet
> not killed; sorrowful, yet always rejoicing; poor, yet
> making many rich; having nothing, and yet possessing
> everything.
>
> 2 CORINTHIANS 6:4-5, 8-10

God promised us His peace because He knew we'd face problems that would threaten to steal that peace from us. He showed us His unwavering and perfect love because He knew we would experience imperfect love, rejection, false accusations, and betrayal at some point in our lives, just as He did.

Yet no matter how bad our situations are, God wants us to know that we *can* survive and that one day the pain will be a distant memory.

So as difficult as things may be right now, hold on. The light has never *not* showed up. Endure the darkness, knowing full well that the sun is on course to return. Nothing will change that. And by the way, nothing will change the Light of the World and His love for you either.

That's something to sing about, isn't it?

If you're not quite ready to sing, at least know that morning is coming. Make the decision to pull the pillow away from your face, push back the comforter, and look for joy in this one new day. And then the next one. And the one after that.

Don't miss the sunrise because you are hiding under the covers. Get up, get out of your emotional bed, and see the promise of a new day.

CHAPTER 40

IT'S YOUR STORY

I now see how owning our story is the bravest thing that we will ever do.
BRENÉ BROWN

As WRITERS, we know there won't be a good novel, film, television drama, or play without a good story.

But what makes a good story?

First, you need a *protagonist* the audience will care about. Your protagonist will deliver, discover, or drive information important to the story because the story is about her.

Your lead cannot take a backseat to another character. She can't hide in the shadows; otherwise it wouldn't be her story. She has to *own* her life. Like it or not, her story is her story.

The most important scenes in the story include the protagonist. These scenes will affect the protagonist in either a positive or a negative way, and if it's a good story, they will ultimately change her in some way. If your protagonist has to overcome incredible obstacles but never learns or grows, then who will care if she achieves her goal in the end?

In every good story, the protagonist will have a goal, and it needs to be something that she will risk everything to achieve. The character may not realize until later in the script that she needs to risk everything, but eventually she realizes how determined she must be to reach her goal.

Someone else in the story also has a goal—your *antagonist*. The pursuit of the antagonist's goal will pit him or her against your protagonist. They both cannot win. Your protagonist must be victorious.

To be interesting and to move your audience emotionally, your story also needs conflict. It may be the protagonist's struggle to face her fears, have faith in her ability to achieve a lifelong dream, right an old wrong, move beyond her past, or wrestle with some other internal conflict.

This internal conflict will cause your protagonist to make a certain decision, and that decision forces her to develop a missing character quality, one she ultimately needs to reach her goal.

Without inner conflict, you do not have an interesting story.

Without growth, you do not have a character and journey the audience will care about.

And the protagonist must struggle to meet her goal. Goals that are easily met do not make good movies or novels. Thus your protagonist needs not only conflict but also complications: obstacles that interfere with her pursuit of the goal. And just when the audience thinks everything is resolved, a few more complications are thrown into the plot.

Complications reveal the strength of the protagonist. Multiple complications prove (to others and to the protagonist) that the heroine's goal is valuable and that she is determined to achieve it.

Complications drive the heroine of your story into action, growth, self-acceptance, surrender, an increased ability to trust, and so many other qualities that everyone needs to survive in life. Complications keep us riveted on a movie. They push the protagonist almost to the breaking point and ultimately to victory. They are why we cheer the result.

Now let's apply this concept of complications to our own life stories. Give us complications in real life, and at the first signs of trouble we're ready to give up, whimper away, and surrender to the antagonist!

Even though we know the power of triumphing over multiple complications and conflict, we want our own stories to be neat and tidy, with no loose ends. Everything must have simple explanations and quick resolutions, and nobody can be injured.

Yet how many of us would sit through a film or read a book in which the protagonist never faced a block wall, encountered an enemy, or suffered setbacks and failure?

We want our lives to be fun and problem-free, with no unpleasant surprises. We want to laugh, not cry. We don't like loss, rejection, and pain. We don't want to endure circumstances that leave us with more questions than answers.

Isn't it that very moment of questioning that intrigues us as we watch good films and read gripping books? Aren't we sitting on the edges of our seats when the heroine reaches the end of her hope and asks, "God, where are you?"

Your story may have taken a turn that doesn't feel at all fun or comfortable. You may be wondering why a God who loves you would allow this chapter or these characters in your story.

But just as with your protagonist, internal growth most likely occurs in the tough times of your life.

Ask people you admire about their stories, and you will hear tales of disappointment, heartache, betrayal, loss, disease, broken relationships, and painful personal growth. Why are they people you admire? Could it be the strength of their character, courage, empathy, or keen sense of humor when times are tough? You can be sure that their stories helped them develop those qualities.

In the same way, God is giving you your story in the middle of your problems, challenges, hurts, and disappointments. Without the hard times, you wouldn't have much of a story. As painful as they are, your story needs them!

And where is God? He's in the midst of your story. He is there *right next to you* in whatever pile-on you had this week, teaching you, training you, and strengthening you. He's peeling off layer after layer of what life has thrown on top of you, telling you to trust Him.

So don't type "The End" while your story is still evolving. Stick with it. Keep adding to your page count. Keep living your story and drawing from it. Because you never know who needs what you're learning right now.

God is giving you *your* story: the parts you want and the parts you would rather not have. But if you hang on, you'll see that He uses all of it! It all comes together in the end, for His glory and your good.

Great "Get Out of Bed" Movies

Hollywood sometimes gets a bad rap. We know there's plenty of garbage out there, but sometimes a movie or television show can be better than any counselor!

Hollywood helped Norman Cousins, a doctor who had been diagnosed with several serious illnesses. He famously lived many more years than anyone predicted he would, and he attributed his longevity to a daily dose of funny movies and TV shows.

He purposefully made time to watch something that made him laugh every single day.

We've known others who found respite from their challenges and built up their courage by watching quality films. When they felt depressed or afraid, when they felt alone or betrayed, when everything seemed hopeless—or even when life was great—they have found inspiration in the power of a good story.

Come to think of it, so have we!

Here are a few of our favorites that have helped us through tough times. They include movies with themes of hope, perseverance, courage, grace, forgiveness, and second chances, as well as movies that will make you laugh and are just plain fun.

You may want to add some of these to your own list.*

They say laughter is the best medicine.

My Big Fat Greek Wedding
The Princess Bride
Groundhog Day
Back to the Future
Enchanted
Home Alone
A Christmas Story

Belting out Broadway show tunes or strapping on your dancing shoes is great too.

Singin' in the Rain
The Music Man
Hello, Dolly!

---

* These movies are rated G, PG, or PG-13 for various reasons. They have enough uplifting or inspirational content that one or both of us felt comfortable recommending them; however, we're aware that everyone's standards are different. And some of them do address more difficult topics. So be sure to read a review and preview them before inviting the kids or grandkids to join you. Find selected reviews at Focus on the Family's Plugged In (pluggedin.com).

Mary Poppins
Summer Stock
Strictly Ballroom

Then again, who doesn't love traveling to another time and place?

Cinderella (Rodgers and Hammerstein—1957, 1965, 1997)
Cinderella (2015)
Pride and Prejudice
Persuasion
Emma
Victoria and Albert
Cranford
The Princess and the Pirate

How about something moving and inspiring?

Chariots of Fire
Bella
Amazing Grace
Pollyanna
To Sir, with Love
Cinderella Man
Les Misérables
Facing the Giants
The Miracle Worker
Lars and the Real Girl
Ice Castles
Follow Me, Boys!
War Room
The Help
The King's Speech

The Englishman Who Went up a Hill But Came down a
  Mountain
A Christmas Carol

Or something that brings out the kid in you?

These particular "children's movies" feature themes of facing
fear, bullies, and challenges with perseverance, as well as finding
forgiveness and a renewed sense of purpose in life. This makes
them *great* for grown-up kids!

A Bug's Life
Finding Nemo
Inside Out
Meet the Robinsons
Monsters University
The Muppets
Up
WALL-E
Wreck-It Ralph

If that doesn't work, you can always try scaring yourself silly.

Arachnophobia, starring Jeff Daniels and John Goodman (Just
  kidding!)

CHAPTER 41

ONE FOOT AND THEN THE OTHER

God is more concerned with conforming me to the likeness of His Son than leaving me in my comfort zones. God is more interested in inward qualities than outward circumstances. Things like refining my faith and humbling my heart, cleaning up my thought life and strengthening my character.

JONI EARECKSON TADA

HAVE YOU CONSIDERED climbing out of bed—or stepping out of the boat, metaphorically speaking—simply because Jesus says, "Come!"?

A few years ago, I (Christin) heard a powerful teaching on Matthew 14:22-33. The pastor pointed out that Jesus isn't confused about our skills or abilities. He doesn't play games with us or set us up to fail. He's not a hard or unreasonable taskmaster. He's the Lover of our Souls and our Savior, Redeemer, and Friend. He has called us to faithfully follow Him and to accomplish His will, the work of His Kingdom here on Earth. He wants us to be successful in that, to fulfill the plans and purposes He has for us.

So any time He asks us to do something, He *always* supplies the power, ability, grace, and strength we need to accomplish whatever it is that He asks us to do. The tools we need actually come *with* the command.

When Jesus asks us to do something, we don't have to wonder *if* we will be able to do it. We know that we can, even if that means walking on water like Peter.

As I consider this idea, I find myself picturing my young nephew, Timmy—the love of my life and apple of my eye! We enjoy doing craft projects together. I was once a teacher, so you can believe me when I say that Timmy is exceptionally handsome, amazingly talented, and incredibly smart. And he has a fabulous personality!

He does have one funny quirk. Every time he's faced with a new challenge or opportunity, Timmy responds with these two words: "I can't."

It's so silly! He loves to learn, play, and create. But before I even hand him the scissors or glue, he declares he can't do whatever I'm about to ask him to do. He hasn't even tried. Most of the time he doesn't even know what the project is. It doesn't matter.

"I can't," he says.

It's like an automatic reflex.

I'm not sure what's at the root of this attitude. It could be a lack of confidence, insecurity, or a fear of failure. He may have inherited some of Auntie's perfectionism: "If I don't think I can do it perfectly the first time, I don't want to try." Or he's embracing some other family members' "Eeyore-ish" perspective on life. Sometimes it's laziness. *That looks like work*, he's probably thinking. *I don't feel like making the effort.*

Regardless, my response is always the same: "Yes, you can!" I'm able to say that because I plan for his success. There

are three things to know about every project I put in front
of Timmy:

1. I chose it specifically for him. I prepared it ahead of time.
   I had a plan and a purpose in mind. I knew before I
   brought it to him that he was fully capable of accomplishing the task, *or* (being a teacher) I knew that he needed
   to learn the skill involved and that this was the way to
   learn it.

2. I have already equipped him. I've prepared him through
   other projects we've worked on together. And I've provided him with all of the supplies and tools he needs
   because I want him to succeed.

3. I'm not going anywhere. I will be right there beside him,
   ready to help every step of the way.

Most of the time, after one or two "I can'ts," Timmy joyfully
discovers that he can. And then we make memories together,
as well as messy craft projects!

Occasionally the "I can'ts" persist. He remains stubborn and
whiny. That's when I smile and say—lovingly, sweetly, firmly—
in my best teacher voice:

"You *can* and you *will*!"

Timmy finally follows my lead, and that leads to success.

Has Jesus called you, as He's called me, to work on a project
with Him?

Let's stop waiting for a sign. Let's stop running, hiding, and
pulling the covers over our heads. We need to stop slumbering,
aka "seeking the Lord in a dream."

Instead, let's step out in obedience and faith.

Some projects He's calling me to do scare me! I find myself suddenly filled with fear, anxiety, insecurity, or doubt. Other projects look like too much effort, too much work.

I start to lift my foot. I might even get it over the side of the bed, but then I tuck it back under the covers.

"I can't! I can't do this. Really, I can't."

Jesus then reminds me that every task He's called me to is one He's chosen and prepared especially for me. He knows that I'm able or I need to be able. He's equipped me with everything I need. And He's right there with me, ready to help every step of the way.

Just the way I am with Timmy.

When I hear myself saying "I can't," it's as if Jesus is gently tipping my chin up and making me look Him right in the eye. I feel Him gazing at me with love and telling me firmly, *Yes, you can. And you will! Let Me help you.*[1]

CHAPTER 42

KEEP CALM AND CARRY ON

Trust the past to God's mercy, the present to God's love, and the future to God's providence.

ATTRIBUTED TO ST. AUGUSTINE

IF YOU ARE STILL READING this book, chances are you've faced mornings when there wasn't enough coffee in the world to get you out of bed.

There wasn't enough chocolate either.

There wasn't even enough money to make you raise your head from that pillow!

There wasn't enough *anything* to help you face the "stuff" of life:

The emotional stuff, the spiritual stuff, the financial stuff. The health and work stuff. The family, the spouse (or lack of spouse), and the kids stuff. The friends and the so-called friends stuff. The church stuff.

The never-ending cycle of news stuff. The "everything's urgent and most of it due yesterday" stuff. The new wrinkles and extra pounds, sagging skin, and hot-flashing stuff. The "new technology changing every five minutes when I'm still hopelessly lost learning the old system" stuff. The "I can't undo it, can't take it back, can't forgive myself, can't forgive them" stuff.

Here's what we've learned about all this stuff: Jesus is enough. He promised He would be more than enough. He's the *enough* we need to get out of bed and do more than survive. He knows exactly what to do with all our "stuff."

Even so, we might be tempted to stay in bed and wait for Him to come back. If we get bored, we can always practice rising to meet Him in the air. (Mattresses are *great* for Rapture practice.)

Then again, we could be waiting a very long time. No one knows the day or time of His return, and it's already been two thousand years.

As much as we like our book title, and try as we might to hurry God's timetable along, we have yet to find any verses in the Bible where Jesus says, "When life gets hard, freak out a little (or a lot, depending) and just curl up in the fetal position until I get back!"

While we've been searching for that Scripture, however, we have found a number of verses in which He said something quite different:

- "Go into all the world."
- "Take courage!"
- "Make every effort."
- "I am with you."

Here's what the prophet Habakkuk declared on one of his "terrible, horrible, no good, very bad" days:

Though the fig tree does not blossom
And there is no fruit on the vines,
Though the yield of the olive fails
And the fields produce no food,
Though the flock is cut off from the fold
And there are no cattle in the stalls,

Yet I will [choose to] rejoice in the LORD;
I will [choose to] shout in exultation in the [victorious] God
    of my salvation!

The Lord GOD is my strength [my source of courage,
    my invincible army];
He has made my feet [steady and sure] like hinds' feet
And makes me walk [forward with spiritual confidence]
    on my high places [of challenge and responsibility].

HABAKKUK 3:17-19, AMP

Even when it seems like there's no earthly reason to rejoice, no reason to have hope, we have *every* reason, and we can make that choice.

We can take one step and then another, in confidence that God is with us. He is working in us and through us. And as we learn to trust Him, our feet will become as fleet—as powerful and graceful—as deer leaping across the mountain heights in answer to His call.

The world looks different from the heights. We've caught glimpses of it. It's a spectacular view that's worth the trip.

We'll keep saying it, because we need to hear it ourselves: Just keep calm, keep your eyes on Jesus, and one day at a time, one step at a time, and one moment at a time, He'll give you the hope, courage, and strength to carry on.

Fifty Things to Do While You're Keeping Calm

Isn't keeping calm challenging enough, you may ask? Do you really need to give us fifty more things to do? Then again, who couldn't use a little inspiration, a little motivation?

These sayings are variations of the ubiquitous "Keep Calm and Carry On" posters that were originally intended to encourage British citizens to persevere through the daunting challenges they faced during World War II.

We're hoping you'll find a new motto or be inspired to create one of your own. It might give you the extra oomph you need to put one foot in front of the other, especially on those days when you're tempted to fall back into bed.

Keep Calm and . . .

1. Never Give Up
2. Laugh Like Crazy
3. Dance in the Rain
4. Be Happy
5. Dream On
6. Eat Bacon
7. Pretend It's Friday
8. Let It Go
9. Add Glitter
10. Just Keep Swimming
11. Pop Bubble Wrap
12. Be Fabulous
13. Make a Difference

14. Keep Moving Forward
15. Squash Spiders
16. Follow the Yellow Brick Road
17. Make It Work
18. Be Yourself
19. Breathe Deeply
20. Love Mason Jars
21. Sing on Mountains
22. Solve the Puzzle
23. Look Busy
24. Change Your Password
25. Wave Like a Princess
26. Pat Yourself on the Back
27. Head for the Spa
28. Look at the Stars
29. Love Your Friends
30. Read Good Books
31. Rock On
32. Shake It Off
33. Live Your Life
34. Count Your Blessings
35. Eat Nutella
36. Ring Carson for Tea
37. Eat Cupcakes
38. Listen to the Sea
39. Do the Limbo
40. Ask Siri
41. Dream Big
42. Stay Strong
43. Have Faith
44. Walk On

45. Turn the Page
46. Trust God
47. Get Your Praise On
48. Pray
49. Put on the Armor of God
50. Keep Your Eyes on Jesus

CHAPTER 43

WHENEVER YOU'RE READY

WE HATE TO OVERWHELM YOU with any more to-dos, but we can't miss one last opportunity to encourage you to let in the light, push back the covers, and take those first few steps out of bed and into a better place.

And we're not talking about heaven! Not yet anyway. No shuffling off this mortal coil until Jesus says you're good and ready. The only shuffling we want to hear is the sound of those bunny-slippered feet on the way to the kitchen for a cup of coffee or tea. (Could you bring us a cup? And some more chocolate, since you seem to be up already.)

Go ahead. We'll wait.

Letting in the Light

Take some time to reflect on the following questions and jot down your answers in a separate notebook (or on the back of your hand or the inside flap of a Netflix envelope—whatever's within easy reach).

1. What's weighing on you right now? Think big things, small things, ordinary and extraordinary, reasonable and unreasonable. Write them all down as fast as you can. Don't filter them!

2. Review the list: What do you notice? What types of things made your list? Are there any common themes or threads? Do you see hints of deeper issues?

3. What can you cross off the list? Delete any past incident you can't change and have no control over as well as anything you're ready to let go of now. See if you can transfer most of the remaining items to your to-do list, your prayer list, or your "think more about this" list. (To think more about it, record your thoughts and questions and then discuss the topic with a friend or counselor.)

4. Pray about each item separately or all of them collectively. Cast your cares (throw back the heavy covers) onto Jesus, because He cares for you. Open and close your hands as you pray to practice letting go of your cares and releasing them to Him. End your prayer time with your hands open to receive everything Jesus has for you: His peace, strength, healing, love, mercy, and grace.

BONUS: Once the caffeine kicks in, take some time to jot down your life story. Include the main points so far, the highs and lows, and what you've been learning in between. E-mail us if you would like to share your story. We'd love to read it! (See our contact information at the end of this book.)

Scriptures for Meditation

He knows the way that I take; when he has tested me,
I will come forth as gold.

JOB 23:10

I waited patiently for the LORD; he turned to me and
heard my cry. He lifted me out of the slimy pit, out of
the mud and mire; he set my feet on a rock and gave me
a firm place to stand. He put a new song in my mouth,
a hymn of praise to our God. Many will see and fear and
put their trust in the LORD.

PSALM 40:1-3

Surely it was for my benefit that I suffered such anguish.
In your love you kept me from the pit of destruction; you
have put all my sins behind your back.

ISAIAH 38:17

Come, let us return to the LORD. He has torn us to pieces
but he will heal us; he has injured us but he will bind up our
wounds. After two days he will revive us; on the third day
he will restore us, that we may live in his presence. Let us
acknowledge the LORD; let us press on to acknowledge him.
As surely as the sun rises, he will appear; he will come to us
like the winter rains, like the spring rains that water the earth.

HOSEA 6:1-3

Prepare your minds for action; be self-controlled; set your
hope fully on the grace to be given you when Jesus Christ
is revealed.

I PETER 1:13

Pushing Back the Covers

Time to think about moving!

If you are experiencing a prolonged season of grief, discouragement, or depression, prayerfully consider creating a plan to reclaim your life. (For help, talk to a trusted friend or counselor and review the recommended resources at the end of this book.)

You can call this activity goal setting, life mapping, or whatever name inspires you. Tools that may help you include a mission statement, an inspirational word for the year, a theme verse, a vision board, a planner, or a list written on a legal pad.

As you brainstorm your goals and how to reach them, first think in terms of what is and is not going well in your life. Next, ask yourself what you could do to move in the right direction.

Finally, break down those ideas into actionable steps. Take time to develop your plan and action list so you don't become overwhelmed.

As you review the list, remember that both God and you play a part in accomplishing your goals. We know God will do His part; He will accomplish those things in our hearts and lives that only He can do. It's up to us to do our part: to make an effort and good choices and to develop the discipline and determination we need to succeed. But even as we do our part, it's actually God's power working in us and through us. He promises that if we ask for His help, He will give it to us.

Martha uses a mission statement to keep her focus: "Life's tough, God's good, and laughter is calorie-free."

Christin chooses a theme word for each year. She then incorporates the word into a paragraph, creating her Scripture-based affirmation and mission statement for the year. Previous years' words have been *courage, obedience, fearless,* and *refuge*.

Write your word or mission statement here:

_____

Feet on the Floor

Try these first steps:

Schedule one fun thing: Take a class or join a group doing something you've always wanted to do or used to love, such as ballroom dancing, singing, acting, painting, pottery, cooking, scrapbooking, running, hiking, horseback riding, or antiquing. Choose an activity that gets you out of the house and reminds you how much better life is outside the walls of your bedroom!

Do one thing to help others: Depending on your health and circumstances, your volunteer assignment could be an ongoing commitment or a one-time event. It may or may not involve prep time or leaving the house.

For instance, you could

- serve in the church nursery;
- volunteer at the local homeless or crisis shelter, animal shelter, food bank, or community center;
- become a Big Brother or Big Sister;
- help build a house for Habitat for Humanity (usually a one-day commitment);
- give blood;
- knit hats or blankets or sew clothing for impoverished children, the ill, or the homeless (find easy patterns on Pinterest);
- teach a Sunday school class or an adult literacy class;

- clean a closet or your pantry and donate unused items;
- greet visitors at church or visit people who have no regular visitors at the hospital or senior living center;
- send Christmas cards to people who might not receive any;
- text your children or grandchildren your prayers for them;
- write notes of encouragement to specific military service members, church missionaries, schoolteachers, friends, or family via social media, e-mail, or snail mail;
- babysit for foster families, single parents, or frazzled young couples;
- post beautiful images, Scriptures, prayers, or other positive, uplifting messages for friends online;
- use your skills to help someone with a project they find overwhelming (for example, help create a budget, organize an office, plan menus, study for a test, etc.); or
- pray faithfully for specific people God brings to mind. If you can, keep in touch with them about their needs and remind them frequently that you are praying for them.

The list is endless! But all you need to do is start with one!

Schedule one health and wellness activity: Make that doctor's appointment you've been putting off or an appointment with a counselor. Sign up for the gym (if you promise you will go this time). Register for an upcoming seminar, conference, or spiritual retreat.

Remember, take baby steps. You can do this! We're cheering you on!

Make Your Own Top Ten Lists

Top Ten Disasters I Feared That Never Came to Pass

1. _____
2. _____
3. _____
4. _____
5. _____
6. _____
7. _____
8. _____
9. _____
10. _____

Top Ten Things I Thought I'd Never Survive, But Did!

1. _____
2. _____
3. _____
4. _____
5. _____
6. _____
7. _____
8. _____
9. _____
10. _____

Top Ten Sassy or Spiritual Comebacks for the Negative Voices in My Head

NEGATIVE VOICE   **COMEBACK**

1. _____   1. _____

2. _____   2. _____

3. _____   3. _____

4. _____   4. _____

5. _____   5. _____

6. _____   6. _____

7. _____   7. _____

8. _____   8. _____

9. _____   9. _____

10. _____   10. _____

Top Ten Favorite Movies That Bring Me Joy, Laughter, or Inspiration

1. _____

2. _____

3. _____

4. _____

5. _____

6. _____

7. _____

8. _____

9. _____

10. _____

Top Ten Songs or Music Videos That Bring Me Joy, Peace, or Hope

1. _____
2. _____
3. _____
4. _____
5. _____
6. _____
7. _____
8. _____
9. _____
10. _____

Top Ten Things That Make Me Happy

(Favorite treats, reads, experiences, activities, or people!)

1. _____
2. _____
3. _____
4. _____
5. _____
6. _____
7. _____
8. _____
9. _____
10. _____

Top Ten Ways Others Can Help Me

(If people want to help me, I'll give them this list of meaningful and supportive ways to do so.)

1. _____
2. _____
3. _____
4. _____
5. _____
6. _____
7. _____
8. _____
9. _____
10. _____

Top Ten Ways I Can Help Others and Be a Blessing to Them

1. _____
2. _____
3. _____
4. _____
5. _____
6. _____
7. _____
8. _____
9. _____
10. _____

Acknowledgments

A GREAT BIG THANK-YOU to the fabulous teams at Focus on the Family and Tyndale House, including Allison Montjoy and LeeAnn Toyer, and especially Larry Weeden, who championed this book from the start. Special thanks to our editor, Julie Holmquist, for her thoughtful guidance and insight.

We also want to thank our families and close friends (both new and lifelong) for their ongoing love and support, for sharing this writer's life with us and being ever ready to offer encouragement and chocolate.

Martha would especially like to thank her husband, Russ, for allowing her to run her first drafts by him even when it interrupted his naps, and for being there through more than four decades of good times and sad times, times of hard-to-understand challenges and times of hard-to-believe blessings.

Christin would especially like to thank her dear friends Kris Camealy and Jennifer Dukes Lee, for their faithful prayers and constant encouragement through the sometimes-crazy process of writing a book, and her husband, Andrew Lazo, for his amazing love, excellent tech support, and brilliant brainstorming in coming up with the subtitle of this one.

Meet the Authors

Martha Bolton is a longtime comedy writer who has written for such performers as Bob Hope, Phyllis Diller, Mark Lowry, and Chonda Pierce. A speaker and an author of more than eighty-eight books of inspiration and humor for all ages, Martha has been nominated for an Emmy, a Writers Guild of America Award, and a Dove Award. This playwright and novelist has also written for singers, politicians, and professional speakers. Learn more at www.MarthaBolton.com.

Christin Ditchfield is an author, a conference speaker, and an internationally syndicated radio host who is passionate about calling women to a deeper life—the kind of life that's found in a deeper relationship with Jesus Christ. For more than twenty-five years, Christin has been encouraging those who love Jesus, teaching them to walk with Him on a daily basis so that they can experience a richer, deeper, more meaningful relationship with Him. She is the author of seventy books, including *What Women Should Know about Letting It Go*. She blogs at www.ChristinDitchfield.com.

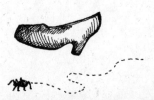

More Help

FOR FACING FEELINGS OF FEAR, ANXIETY, DISCOURAGEMENT, AND DEPRESSION

Bolton, Martha. *Ouch! Encouragement for the Hurts of Life*. The Exclamation Series. West Monroe, LA: Howard, 2010.

Cowman, L. B. *Streams in the Desert: 366 Daily Devotional Readings*. Edited by Jim Reimann. Grand Rapids, MI: Zondervan, 2008.

Ditchfield, Christin. *What Women Should Know about Facing Fear: Finding Freedom from Anxious Thoughts, Nagging Worries, and Crippling Fears*. Abilene, TX: Leafwood, 2013.

———. *What Women Should Know about Letting It Go: Breaking Free from the Power of Guilt, Discouragement, and Defeat*. Abilene, TX: Leafwood, 2015.

Vernick, Leslie. *Lord, I Just Want to Be Happy*. Eugene, OR: Harvest House, 2009.

Yancey, Philip. *What's So Amazing about Grace?* Rev. ed. Grand Rapids, MI: Zondervan, 2002.

FOR FACING PEOPLE AND RELATIONSHIP ISSUES

Bevere, John. *The Bait of Satan: Living Free from the Deadly Trap of Offense*. 20th anniversary ed. Lake Mary, FL: Charisma House, 2014.

Carlson, Dwight L., MD. *Overcoming Hurts and Anger: Finding Freedom from Negative Emotions*. Eugene, OR: Harvest House, 2000.

Cloud, Dr. Henry, and Dr. John Townsend. *Boundaries: When to Say Yes, How to Say No to Take Control of Your Life*. Grand Rapids, MI: Zondervan, 1992.

Coughlin, Paul, and Jennifer D. Degler. *No More Christian Nice Girl: When Just Being Nice—Instead of Good—Hurts You, Your Family, and Your Friends*. Bloomington, MN: Bethany House, 2010.

Fore, Jo Ann. *When a Woman Finds Her Voice: Overcoming Life's Hurts and Using Your Story to Make a Difference*. Abilene, TX: Leafwood, 2013.

Frangipane, Francis. *The Stronghold of God: Finding God's Place of Immunity from Attacks of the Enemy*. Lake Mary, FL: Charisma House, 1998.

Lotz, Anne Graham. *Wounded by God's People: Discovering How God's Love Heals Our Hearts.* Grand Rapids, MI: Zondervan, 2013.

Nelson, Tommy, and Steve Leavitt. *Walking on Water When You Feel Like You're Drowning: Finding Hope in Life's Darkest Moments.* Colorado Springs: Focus on the Family, 2012.

Rapson, James, and Craig English. *Anxious to Please: Seven Revolutionary Practices for the Chronically Nice.* Naperville, IL: Sourcebooks, 2006.

Rutherford, Dudley. *Walls Fall Down: Seven Steps from the Battle of Jericho to Overcome Any Challenge.* Nashville: Nelson, 2014.

Stoker, John R. *Overcoming Fake Talk: How to Hold REAL Conversations That Create Respect, Build Relationships, and Get Results.* New York: McGraw-Hill Education, 2013.

Stone, Douglas, Bruce Patton, and Sheila Heen. *Difficult Conversations: How to Discuss What Matters Most.* New York: Viking Penguin, 1999.

Vernick, Leslie. *The Emotionally Destructive Relationship: Seeing It, Stopping It, Surviving It.* Eugene, OR: Harvest House, 2007.

Yager, Jan. *When Friendship Hurts: How to Deal with Friends Who Betray, Abandon, or Wound You.* New York: Fireside, 2002.

FOR FACING THE PAIN OF GRIEF AND LOSS

Birdseye, Sue. *When Happily Ever After Shatters: Seeing God in the Midst of Divorce and Single Parenting.* Colorado Springs: Focus on the Family, 2013.

Brestin, Dee. *The God of All Comfort: Finding Your Way into His Arms.* Grand Rapids, MI: Zondervan, 2009.

Dobson, James C. *When God Doesn't Make Sense: Holding On to Your Faith during the Hardest Times.* Carol Stream, IL: Tyndale, 2012.

Guthrie, David and Nancy Guthrie. *When Your Family's Lost a Loved One: Finding Hope Together.* Colorado Springs: Focus on the Family, 2008.

Lewis, C. S. *A Grief Observed.* New York: HarperCollins, 2015.

Lyons, David, and Linda Lyons Richardson. *Don't Waste the Pain: Learning to Grow through Suffering.* Colorado Springs: NavPress, 2010.

Roper, Gayle. *A Widow's Journey: Reflections on Walking Alone.* Eugene, OR: Harvest House, 2015.

Yancey, Philip. *Where Is God When It Hurts?* Grand Rapids, MI: Zondervan, 2002.

FOR FACING LIFE—AND GETTING YOURS BACK!

Bolton, Martha. *The Whole World Is Changing and I'm Too Hot to Care.* Atlanta: Elk Lake Publishing, 2015.

Brestin, Dee. *Idol Lies: Facing the Truth about Our Deepest Desires.* Brentwood, TN: Worthy, 2012.

Feinberg, Margaret. *Fight Back with Joy: Celebrate More. Regret Less. Stare Down Your Greatest Fears.* Brentwood, TN: Worthy, 2015.

Kent, Carol. *Unquenchable: Grow a Wildfire Faith That Will Endure Anything.* Grand Rapids, MI: Zondervan, 2014.

Kent, Carol, and Jennie Afman Dimkoff. *Miracle on Hope Hill: And Other True Stories of God's Love.* New York: Howard Books, 2011.

Lee, Jennifer Dukes. *The Happiness Dare: Pursuing Your Heart's Deepest, Holiest, and Most Vulnerable Desire.* Carol Stream, IL: Tyndale, 2016.

Whitwer, Glynnis. *Taming the To-Do List: How to Choose Your Best Work Every Day.* Grand Rapids, MI: Revell, 2015.

Notes

PART ONE: FACING YOUR FEELINGS WHEN YOU'D RATHER HIDE
1. Earl Nightingale, "The Fog of Worry (Only 8% of Worries Are Worth It)," from *The Essence of Success*, accessed January 15, 2013, http://www.nightingale.com /articles/the-fog-of-worry-only-8-of-worries-are-worth-it.
2. Heather Thompson, "12 Life Lessons from Mister Rogers," *Parade*, accessed December 30, 2016, http://parade.com/379451/hthompson/12-life-lessons-from -mister-rogers/.
3. Helen Keller, *The Open Door* (New York: Doubleday, 1957), 17.
4. Susan Bogert Warner and Edwin Othello Excell, "Jesus Bids Us Shine," 1868.

PART TWO: FACING PEOPLE WHEN YOU'D RATHER RUN
1. Oswald Chambers, *The Love of God: An Intimate Look at the Father-Heart of God* (Grand Rapids, MI: Discovery House, 2015), n.p.
2. Dr. Henry Cloud and Dr. John Townsend, *Boundaries: When to Say Yes, How to Say No to Take Control of Your Life* (Grand Rapids, MI: Zondervan, 1992), 112.

PART THREE: FACING LOSS WHEN IT'S NOT ON THE AGENDA
1. Dietrich Bonhoeffer, *Letters and Papers from Prison* (Minneapolis: Fortress Press, 2010), 50–51.
2. Rev. C. H. Spurgeon, *Gleanings among the Sheaves* (New York: Sheldon and Company, 1869), 41.
3. Johnson Oatman, Jr., "Count Your Blessings," 1897.
4. Excerpted in part from *A Thankful Heart* by Christin Ditchfield (Ventura, CA: Regal, 2012), n.p.
5. Johnson Oatman, Jr., "Count Your Blessings," 1897.

PART FOUR: FACING LIFE—AND GETTING YOURS BACK!
1. Chapter excerpted in part from *What Women Should Know about Letting It Go: Breaking Free from the Power of Guilt, Discouragement, and Defeat* by Christin Ditchfield (Abilene, TX: Leafwood, 2015), 174–75.